THE
BEE-KEEPER'S MANUAL

By Henry Taylor

THE BEE-KEEPER'S MANUAL,

OR

PRACTICAL HINTS
ON THE
MANAGEMENT AND COMPLETE PRESERVATION
OF
THE HONEY-BEE;

WITH
A DESCRIPTION OF THE MOST APPROVED HIVES,
AND OTHER APPURTENANCES OF THE APIARY.

ILLUSTRATED BY NUMEROUS ENGRAVINGS.

Contents

**PREFACE
TO
THE FOURTH EDITION.**

Twelve years have elapsed since the original publication of the Bee-keeper's Manual. For the fourth time the author is called upon to revise his little book, and he still thinks that the leading object in offering it to public notice will best be explained in the words with which it was first introduced. "The existence of the following pages had its origin, some time ago, in the request of a friend, that the author would give him a brief practical compendium of the management of Bees, on the humane or depriving system. Similar applications came from other quarters. The subject is one which has of late acquired increased interest; but the hints following would perhaps never have been prepared for the press, had not the hours of a protracted confinement by illness required some diversity of occupation and amusement. On reviewing his experience as an amateur bee-keeper, the author was led to believe that the result of it, added to a concise view of such particulars as are usually spread over a large surface in works of this nature, and arranged according to the progressive order of the seasons, might be useful to others, seeking like himself occasional relaxation from weightier matters in watching over and protecting these interesting and valuable insects. Step by step this or that defect of construction in his Hives had been remedied, and such conveniences added as necessity or the spirit of improvement from time to time had suggested. These are briefly described in the following little work. If it have the good fortune, though in a small degree, to smooth the path (usually a rough and uncertain one) of the apiarian novice,—of removing ignorance and prejudice, or of obviating any portion of the difficulties with which a more general cultivation of bees has to contend,—why may not the contribution of this mite be considered a humble addition to the store of USEFUL KNOWLEDGE?"

In its present renewed form, the author has been induced partially to extend his first design (originally much restricted in its scope), by entering somewhat more at large into the subject of Bee management, and the general details of practice. Although not professing to offer his remarks to any particular class of readers, he is, nevertheless, inclined to think they will frequently be found, in an especial degree, applicable to the position of the amateur Apiarian. For the peculiar use of cottage bee-keepers, tracts and scraps innumerable have been issued,—probably with very uncertain effect. In short, there is little room for doubt that these can be more effectually benefited by example and verbal advice, than by any kind of printed instructions. Be this as it may, putting out of the question the long train of contingencies incident to locality, season, &c., much must often be left to individual judgment and careful observation; and no writer can be expected to meet every supposable case of difficulty in dealing with insects confessedly often so intractable as bees. The author, therefore, must be considered as merely laying down a scheme of general recommendations; aiming much less at novelty than at plain practical utility; not hesitating occasionally to borrow the language of other unexceptionable authorities where it clearly expressed his convictions, or coincided with the results of his own experience; but carefully abstaining from any interference with the dogmatists and hyper-critics in the settlement of the affairs of their peculiar vocation.

If some of the details relative to the construction of hives or their appurtenances appear to be tedious to the general reader, it must be borne in mind that these are chiefly addressed to the mechanic, who will not be found to object that his particular department has received the aid of a careful attention to matters of description and direction.

On the whole, the author is induced to hope that the improved arrangement, additional information, and variety of illustration now introduced, will render superfluous any apology for a small unavoidable increase in the size of the book.

April, 1850.

PREFACE

TO

THE FIFTH EDITION.

In once more revising the following pages for republication, the author has still kept in view the purpose in which they originated, as referred to in a former preface, and which is again prefixed. He trusts that the intervening period has not been unprofitably occupied in the task of continued investigation and experiment relative to the general economy of the Bee; in the introduction either of original invention or improvement as regards the mechanical requirements of the Apiary; and in maturing the many useful suggestions derived in the course of a pretty widely extended correspondence. The incorporation of matter thus arising must be the apology, if such is needed, for the omission or abridgment, here and there, of some that a later experience had superseded or modified. From these causes the rewriting of many portions of the work became a necessity, together with the introduction of much new illustration,—on the whole resulting in a slightly enlarged volume. Under the circumstances of accumulated materials, condensation was often found more difficult of accomplishment than expansion, had this been thought desirable; but brevity throughout has been the aim, so far as seemed consistent with clear explanation and obvious utility. A work on the Honey-Bee, thus restricted in its object and scope almost entirely to details of a practical bearing, may not entitle it to much literary or scientific consideration, but—without reference to the claims involved in a large circulation—the author will never regret the time and thought bestowed, where the leading aim was the welfare and preservation of one of the most curious of God's creatures; and the dissemination of knowledge in relation to a pursuit in rural life, of more general interest, probably, than many kindred ones of higher pretensions.

August, 1855.

PREFACE

TO

THE SIXTH EDITION.

A continued, or rather an increasing sale of the Bee-keeper's Manual has, for the sixth time, rendered a reprint necessary; confirming the belief that a work, first appearing as the amusement of an idle hour, has, in its more recent extended form, not been unappreciated, as supplying a medium between the costly treatises of elaborate investigators and compilers and the class of mere tracts on Bee management, that have, with more or less of pretension, abounded of late years. These are sometimes directed to detached points or portions only in the wide and diversified field of controversy opened in relation to the Honey-Bee, or confined by space to the usual desultory scraps of information for the guidance of the inexperienced tyro, or supposed cottager; communicating just enough to prove the necessity of advancing a step further, by consulting works that take a wider and more systematic view of the subject in its details. The prefaces to the two last editions of the book are again placed before the reader, as showing that, in its successive stages, the author's purpose has been the condensation of a large amount of useful apiarian knowledge, assisted by an unusual variety of illustration. The present republication professedly follows in the path of its predecessors; such additional matter or remark being occasionally introduced as space permitted, and the onward progress of improvement appeared to demand.

May, 1860.

What well appointed Commonwealths! where each Adds to the stock of happiness for all; Wisdom's own forums! where professors teach Eloquent lessons in their vaulted hall: Galleries of art, and schools of industry! Stores of rich fragrance! Orchestras of song! What marvellous seats of hidden alchymy! How oft, when wandering far and erring long, Man might learn Truth and Virtue from the Bee!   Bowring.

THE
BEE-KEEPER'S MANUAL.

The Hive or domestic Honey Bee of this country is classed entomologically *Apis mellifica*, order *Hymenoptera*, as having four wings.[A] The limits to which a Bee-keeper's Manual of practice is necessarily confined, permits only the remark that these extraordinary insects are, as to origin and history, lost in the mists of a remote antiquity. We know, however, that they, their habits and productions, are alluded to in Scripture, and attracted marked attention and admiration in the early eastern communities, where doubtless was familiar their characteristic Oriental name, *Deburah,*—"she that speaketh." Subsequently, the bee has spread itself, or been carried, in spite of clime and temperature, over a large portion of the old continents; following in the wake of civilized man wherever he has placed his foot in the primeval forests of the new world; and later on, in our own time, has been received as a friend and benefactor in the boundless regions of Australasia and the islands of the Pacific Ocean. From the time of Aristotle down to our own day, treatises on Bees have ever been popular, and the curious naturalist has no difficulty in collecting a library relative to a subject apparently inexhaustible. But space allows us to notice neither the crude speculations to be met with in ancient literature, the unprofitable disputations too often prevailing among modern Bee-annalists, nor the endless catalogue of hives, possible and impossible, of every period, by which the novice is bewildered. Our present purpose is restricted to a utilitarian view of the subject of apiarian knowledge, where science, invention, and the most competent testimony, have combined to place it in our own day.

[A] Although in the following pages the *Apis mellifica* alone is referred to, it may be well here to state that attention has recently been directed, not only in our own country, but in a still higher degree in Germany, France, and even in the United States of America, to the introduction of the Ligurian Bee, or *Apis Ligustica* of Italy, the race most probably that was known to Aristotle and Virgil, and, perhaps, to the ancient Greeks. The combs of this species of bee closely resemble those of the common kind, but its outward characteristics exhibit a marked difference; the first rings of the abdomen being of a reddish colour, instead of dark brown. A fertile Ligurian queen is readily accepted in an English stock-hive, from which a common queen has been abstracted, and in due time young Italians are distinguishable, gradually displacing the original inhabitants. Report speaks favorably of the superiority of the strangers over our own bee, as more hardy, more laborious, less irascible, and as swarming earlier.

To those who may be unacquainted with the leading characteristic of the Honey Bee, it is necessary to premise that in every family, when fully constituted, its members are of three kinds of individuals; viz.,

A *Queen*, or *Mother Bee*,

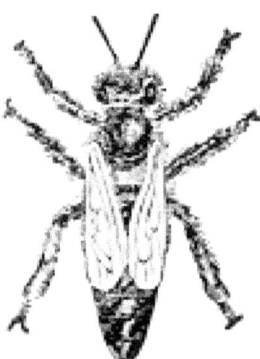

The *Common*, or *Working Bees*;

And (during a part of the year) the *Male*, or *Drone Bees*.

Thus associated, they severally perform their allotted functions in great harmony, labouring for the general good, combining in self-defence, recognising one another, but permitting the intrusion of no stranger within the hive.

THE QUEEN OR MOTHER BEE

Is darker on the back, longer, and more taper towards the end of her body than the common bees; has longer legs but shorter wings, and is of a tawny or yellowish-brown colour underneath. She is supreme in the hive, admitting no rival or equal; and is armed with a sting, somewhat more curved in form than that of the common bees, which, however, she rarely uses. Where she goes the other bees follow; and so indispensable is her presence to the existence of the commonwealth, that where she is not none will long remain. She is the mother of the entire community, her office being to lay the eggs from which all proceed, whether future queens, drones, or workers. Separate her from the family, and she instinctively resents the injury, refuses food, pines, and dies. Without a Queen, or a prospect of one, the labour of the hive is suspended, and a gradual dispersion or emigration of the community ensues.

Those who have examined the appearance of a bee-hive, after it has been filled with combs during a year, will recollect seeing suspended here and there, certain small inverted cup-shaped forms. These are the partially destroyed remains of what were designed for the birthplaces of young queens, and so-called royal cells or cradles. They are much larger than the common hexagonal cells in which the working bees are bred; varying also in their composition, the material of which appears to be a mixture of wax or propolis, and the farina of flowers. Soon after the foundation of one of them has been laid, an egg is deposited in it, the work of completion of the cradle being carried on as required by the increasing growth of its occupant. When finished and closed up, it presents in form the appearance of an oblong spheroid, about an inch long, usually appended like a stalactite perpendicularly to the edge of a comb, the small end or mouth being downwards, a position most favorable to economy of space in the hive. In number the royal cells vary from four or five to a dozen, and sometimes more. They are not peopled till after the usual great spring laying of eggs for the production of working bees, preparatory to swarming; and also those to produce drone bees. The existence of the latter, or in some stage towards existence, is an invariable preliminary to the construction of royal cells, the reason for which will hereafter appear. The affectionate attachment evinced by the nurse-bees towards the royal larvæ is marvellous, the quantity of food given is profuse, and they arrive severally at maturity on or about the sixteenth day from the laying of each egg; these having usually an interval between them of but a few days. Of the young females or princesses, as they are often called, and the mode of disposing of supernumerary ones, we shall speak more at large when we come to treat of swarming. The duration of life in a Queen bee, under ordinary circumstances, is, by a wise provision for the perpetuation of the species, much more prolonged than is the case with the common bees, and some observers have imagined that it may in some instances have reached to nearly five years. So far as my knowledge extends, the oldest queen bee of which we have an authentic record, existed, in the apiary of Mr. Robert Golding,[B] during the space of three years and eleven months. She died in April or May, showing little sign of decrepitude, judging by her fertility, for previously she had filled the hive with an abundance of brood of every kind. I am, however, inclined to believe that a Queen is oftener changed than we are always aware of, for in nothing in Nature is there displayed a more careful attention to the due preservation of a family of bees than in the provision made for supplying the casual vacancies arising not merely from the natural demise of the sovereign, but from other causes, especially those involving deficient powers or absolute sterility. I should, therefore, discountenance any attempt at direct interference by the forcible removal of a queen, after a prescribed period, as has sometimes been advocated. If, however, it should happen that such removal is absolutely necessary, the bees will accept a successor as soon as they have discovered their loss, which is often not till after the lapse of several hours. If all is right the previous agitation will cease.

[B] See the 'Shilling Bee-book,' by Robert Golding.

And this leads us on to a curious, if not unique fact in relation to the natural history of the Honey bee, which though probably not unknown to the ancients, was rediscovered and promulgated by Schirach, a member of an apiarian society, formed in the middle of the last century at Little Bautzen, in Upper Lusatia. In contradistinction to the usual way in which a young Queen is created, preparatory to the swarming season, by what is denominated the *natural* process, the details we are about to give show that the same thing may be effected by another mode, or, as it is said, *artificially*. Whether these terms, as opposed to each other, are rightly applied or not, they at least mark a difference; and being thus practically understood, we shall follow the example of other authors in using them. The fact itself, startling as at first it seemed, has been so clearly authenticated, that any lurking scepticism has disappeared; and, indeed, the principle is now so well understood and carried into general use by the scientific Apiculturist that, in a popular treatise on the Honey bee, our object would he imperfectly accomplished without entering into a few particulars in connection with it. And first, we have the assurance that the prevalent opinion as to any supposed original or generated difference between common eggs and those laid for the especial production of Queen bees, is founded in error; an altered and accelerated mode as to the development of the egg being all that is needed for the maturation of a perfect female. That we may understand the method of procedure on the part of the bees, we have to suppose that a hive has been deprived of its Queen (no matter whether by death or design) at that particular period when eggs and larvæ are each present in the cells of the combs: such larvæ being not more than two or three days old, for this is essential. Could we at such a juncture witness the proceedings of the family, a spectacle would be presented of much domestic distress and confusion when it had been discovered that the hive was queenless. Soon, however, the scene changes to the quietude of hope, for the foundation of a queen's cell (and as a provision against possible failure, often of three or four) is commenced by the bees, usually within twenty-four hours. They select a common grub or larva, and enlarge the cell it occupies, by sacrificing the three contiguous ones, surrounding it with a cylindrical enclosure; the new cradle of royalty presenting in this stage the appearance of an acorn cup. The embryo Princess, for such she has now become, is amply supplied with a nurture, supposed to differ from that given to the common larvæ (a point questioned by some naturalists); her habitation in the meanwhile receiving elongation to suit her growth. About the fifth day the worm assumes the nymph state, the cell being now worked into its usual pear-shaped figure; the bees quitting it as soon as the lower end is finally closed. About the fourteenth day a perfectly developed female comes forth, in no respect differing from a Queen bred in the natural way. Fecundation and the laying of eggs usually follow in a few days, the economy of the hive then resuming its wonted course.

The Queen bee rarely leaves home, or is to be seen, except in hives constructed purposely with a view to observation. In such a one I have frequently watched the proceedings, as she has leisurely traversed the combs, the bees clearing a passage on her approach, their heads turned towards her, and, by repeatedly touching her with their antennæ, showing a marked attachment, a favour she is occasionally seen to return. Indeed, in some well-authenticated instances, affection has been continued even after her death. The great object of her existence being the perpetuation of the species, her majesty seems intent on nothing more, during these royal progresses, than peeping into the cells as she passes them, ever and anon selecting one, within which she inserts her abdomen, and deposits at the bottom an egg. These are about the size of those produced by a butterfly, but more elongated, and of a bluish-white colour. So prolific are some Queens that I have sometimes witnessed an extraordinary waste of eggs when, as the combs have become in great part filled with brood or honey, she finds a difficulty in meeting with a sufficiency of unoccupied cells. In such an emergency, impelled by necessity, the eggs are dropped at random, and carried off or devoured by the bees. No doubt an early and productive season tends often to this result, and marks the necessity of a timely temporary addition to the storing room of the family. The great laying takes place in April and May, when the number of eggs has been variously estimated by naturalists at 200 to 600 in a day, amounting to an aggregate of 50,000 to 80,000 in the year. "This sounds like a great number," remarks Dr. Bevan,[C] "but it is much exceeded by some other insects." Indeed, a wider calculation has been made, in his valuable remarks on bees, by the Rev. Dr. W. Dunbar,[D] who thinks that some Queens (for they are not all equally prolific) produce 100,000 eggs yearly. When we take into account the enormous demand for the supply of swarms, the constant deaths in the course of nature, and the thousands of lives always sacrificed by casualties of various kinds, at home and abroad, I am inclined to lean to the higher estimate. No doubt as the cold weather advances there is a considerable falling off in the number of eggs, but the interval is very short in which the queen, in a flourishing hive, discontinues laying more or less. "Indeed," observes Mr. Golding, "it appears that at any time when the temperature is not too low for the bees to appropriate the food that is given to them, the Queen will deposit eggs."

[C] See 'The Honey-Bee, its Natural History, Physiology, and Management.' By Edward Bevan, M.D.

[D] See the 'Naturalist's Library,' vol. xxxiv.

THE COMMON OR WORKING BEES

Are the least in size, and in point of numbers in a family are variously calculated at twelve to thirty thousand, according to the bulk of the swarm; though under certain circumstances they are sometimes much more numerous. As regards sex, we have seen in the preceding section that there is no reason to doubt they are females, only that the reproductive organs and ovaries are not as fully developed as they are in the case of a perfect Queen; and this has led to the erroneous use of the term *neuters*, as sometimes applied to the common bees. If any doubt should remain as to their sex, it is removed by the knowledge that, in some rare instances, they have been able to produce eggs. Like the Queen, each has the power of stinging. The use of the sting, however, usually involves a loss of life, for, being barbed like an arrow, the bee has rarely the power of withdrawing it.

The eggs for workers are deposited in the common cells in the centre of the hive, being the part first selected for that purpose, the Queen usually laying them equally on each side of a comb, and nearly back to back. In four or five days' time, they are hatched, when a small worm is presented, remaining in the larva or grub state four to six days more, during which period it is assiduously fed by the nurse-bees. The larvæ then assume the nymph or pupa form, and spin themselves a film or cocoon, the nurses immediately after sealing them up with a substance which Huber[E] calls wax. It is, however, a mixture of wax and pollen, being thicker, more highly coloured, more porous, and less tenacious, probably to afford air, and facilitate the escape of the imprisoned tenant. This takes place about the twenty-first day from the laying of the egg, unless the process has been somewhat retarded by cold weather. The attentive observer may at this time, in a suitable hive, witness the struggles and scrambling into the world, generally by its own exertions, of the now perfect *imago*, the little grey new-born shaking, brushing, and smoothing itself, preparatory to entering upon the duties of life, and in a day or two, or sooner, it is busily occupied in the fields.[F]

[E] See "Observations on the Natural History of Bees," by Francis Huber; English edition, London, 1841. An invaluable work to the scientific apiculturist.

[F] As soon as the young bee comes forth, the others partially clear the cell, and it again receives an egg; this being often repeated four or five times in the season. Afterwards the cells become the receptacles for honey or farina; but they are found in time to become contracted or thickened by this rapid succession of tenants, and the consequent deposits of exuviæ, excrement, &c. It has been asserted by Huber and other naturalists, that young bees, bred in old contracted cells, are proportionately smaller in size. Such combs should be removed from the hive.

Though we have, as I conceive, no actual proof that the occupation of individual bees is at all times unchangeably directed to one point (as some naturalists have imagined), observation shows that the division of labour is one of their leading characteristics. Some are engaged in secreting and elaborating wax for the construction of combs in the hive; others in warming the eggs; in feeding the larvæ, as also their queen; in ventilating and cleansing the hive; in guarding and giving notice of attacks or annoyance from without; and the rest in searching the fields and woods for the purpose of collecting honey and farina, for present and future store.

The longevity of the working bees has often furnished matter for dispute, and erroneous ideas have been engendered where a family has been seen for a series of years to continue in a populous and thriving condition. But during this period the Queen (or more than one in succession) has been incessantly occupied in laying eggs innumerable, to supply by new births the place of the countless thousands of bees that periodically disappear. Their dwelling has remained, but successive generations of tenants have kept its works in repair, giving way in time to fresh occupants. It is shown clearly by Dr. Bevan and other good authorities, both by argument and actual experiment, that six to eight months is the limit of their duration; for, notwithstanding the immense annual increase, the numbers in a hive dwindle down gradually, owing to the chills of autumn and towards the end of the year, to a comparatively few. There is no doubt, therefore, that every bee existing after Christmas was bred during the latter part of the summer or autumn; and this is a sufficient answer to those who sometimes inquire what is to become of the accumulated masses of bees, in hives managed on the depriving system, where neither swarming nor destruction takes place.

We might here allude to a prevalent error as to any inherent difference, local or otherwise, in the characteristics of the domestic Honey bee. When we hear it said, that some are "better workers" than others, all that ought to be understood is, that the family has the advantage of being under favorable circumstances as to locality or season; with a fertile Queen, and an abundant population, for without these essentials, every operation goes on sluggishly, and prosperity becomes hopeless.

THE DRONE OR MALE BEES

Are computed in the early part of the summer at one to two thousand, and upwards, in a stock hive; but the numbers are irregular, for a weak stock will often have an undue proportion. They possess no sting; are larger, darker, and more hairy than the common bees; easily distinguishable by their heavy motion on the wing, and by their louder humming or *droning*.

After her great spring laying of common eggs has far advanced, and as an invariable preliminary to the construction of royal cells, the Queen proceeds to deposit eggs intended for the production of drones or males, though often without discontinuing those for workers. The drone eggs are laid in cells larger in diameter, and stronger than the others, and usually placed towards the outer extremities of the hive.[G] A longer period is necessary for the development of a male than a female, and the drones pass through their various stages in about twenty-four to twenty-six days, being seldom seen till about the beginning of May (though occasionally earlier), and then only in warm weather, in the middle of the day. These are the produce of the first-laid eggs; for a second smaller laying of drone eggs commonly takes place about two months later, though the males are rarely found after August, unless under certain contingencies.

[G] A curious question for the naturalist arises as to the instinct which directs a Queen bee invariably to deposit the proper eggs in the proper cells. The most accurate microscopic observation cannot detect any difference between the egg of a worker, that of a drone, or of a Queen, all proceeding indiscriminately from the same ovaries and oviduct. Ingenious theories have been advanced as to the possibility of what some call impregnated and unimpregnated eggs being laid at the option of the Mother bee. Huber's opinion, "that nature does not allow the Queen the choice of the eggs she is to lay," only adds to the difficulty of arriving at any satisfactory conclusion.

The drones take no part in the collection of stores, nor in any operation or process of the hive, for which they have proverbially suffered much ignorant and absurd reproach, since Nature has denied them the necessary means, and in their creation has allotted them a distinct office. Indeed, their flights from the hive are only occasional short ones, and they rarely alight during such excursions. They are of the male sex, their presence in a hive being only required at that particular period when the young queens are arriving at maturity; for of all the theories that have been entertained as to the functions of the drones, that of Huber is undoubtedly the true one,—impregnation.

"Naturalists," says Huber, "have been extremely embarrassed to account for the number of males in most hives, and which seem only a burden on the community, since they appear to fulfil no function. But we now begin to discern the object of nature in multiplying them to such an extent. As fecundation cannot be accomplished within the hive, and as the queen is obliged to traverse the expanse of the atmosphere, it is requisite that the males should be numerous, that she may have the chance of meeting some one of them. Were only two or three in each hive, there would be little probability of their departure at the same instant with the Queen, or that they would meet in their excursions; and most of the females might thus remain sterile."

Were any doubt to remain on the subject, perhaps the annual destruction of the drones by the workers throws the most satisfactory light on the design of their creation. This process varies in point of time, according to circumstances. Deprive a hive forcibly of its Queen, and, according to Bonner and Huber, no expulsion of drones takes place. "In such cases," says the latter, "they are tolerated and fed, and many are seen even in the middle of January." They are retained under the inspiration of hope, for a contingency might arise to require their presence. Where a necessity for swarming has been in any way superseded, there are either no royal cells constructed, or the young queens meet with premature destruction. Then frequently commences an early expulsion of the drones, thus rendered purposeless: they become mere consumers, an incumbrance in the hive, and as such the common bees instinctively wage fierce war upon them, ending in total annihilation: nor are even the male larvæ allowed to remain in their cells. This expulsive process often commences, under such circumstances, in the middle, or at any rate towards the end of May, as I have repeatedly witnessed, and not unfrequently is again resorted to later on in the season. On the other hand, in the case of swarming hives it does not take place till July, or even later, according to season and locality, when all the royal brood is disposed of. The circumstances differ in the two cases; and the bees in this, as in other parts of their practice, are sufficiently utilitarians to modify their proceedings accordantly. In the one instance, the office of the males is rendered void, and in the other it is indispensable to the young queens. Such of these as go forth with swarms become fertilized in two or three days after (though sometimes it is later than this), followed by the laying of eggs in about a similar distance of time. Thenceforth they remain fruitful, if not ever after (as is the case with some other insects), at all events for a year, for young bees are produced, without the subsequent presence of a single male in the family, till the following spring. The destruction of the drones, therefore, be it sooner or later, may be considered an indication that the hive contains no queen brood, and, consequently, that no swarming is to be expected.

Conflicting opinions have been formed as to the desirableness of assisting the working bees in the task of expelling the drones—often a protracted process—for although the latter are not armed, like their more numerous opponents, yet their superior size and strength dispose them often to make a stout resistance. If it can be done at once, without undue annoyance to the family, much fighting and valuable time may doubtless be saved by interfering; but no advice can be worse than that of attempting to accomplish the work piecemeal. When attacked, the drones, to stave off the impending storm, will congregate together in a remote part of the hive. Observation led me to think they would at such a time be glad to retreat for still greater safety into a separate box, so placed as to be accessible to them. Accordingly, on the 14th of June, in one of my collateral stock-hives, where the drones for a day or two had been hard pushed by the others, I opened a communication on the ground floor into an empty side box. My theory was completely realised, for the poor drones gladly made their way into this, where they remained clustered at the top like a swarm, not a single common bee accompanying them, and would probably have been starved. The following morning I took away the box of drones and destroyed them, counting rather more than 2200, besides some few that had escaped; altogether a greater number than the usual estimate gives to a family. I did not find among them a solitary working bee; nor could I discover in the parent stock-hive one remaining drone. The bees peaceably at once recommenced work, and did well; as if glad in this wholesale way to be rid of their late unprofitable inmates. What was the cost of their daily maintenance? And what proportion to the entire population of the hive did the drones bear? After this apparently large abstraction, no sensible difference was observable in the crowding. In this hive the usual second laying of drone eggs took place, and a good many more drones were expelled at the end of July. I have not been enabled to repeat this experiment, but have no doubt it would always succeed under similar circumstances.

SWARMING (OR SINGLE HIVING) AND DEPRIVING SYSTEMS.

The multiplication of families or colonies of bees, in the natural manner, is accomplished by the secession of a portion of the inhabitants of a stock-hive, which has become over-peopled, with insufficient room for the breeding and storing departments. This act of emigration or swarming is sometimes an affair of expediency only; and by a timely enlargement and decrease in the temperature of the hive it may often be prevented. As soon as warm weather sets in, a common sized hive becomes crowded and heated to excess; and at length a separation of the family becomes a matter of necessity. In anticipation of this event, royal cells are constructed and tenanted for the rearing of young queens, for without these no swarming occurs. A crowded dwelling therefore naturally prompts to this preliminary; whilst on the contrary, a large hive has the effect of retarding the formation of such cells, and the migration of which they are the precursor. In the words of Gelieu,[H] "in the swarming season the strong hives are almost entirely filled with brood-combs. At that time also honey becomes abundant; and when fine days succeed each other, the working bees amass an astonishing quantity. But where is it to be stored? Must they wait till the young bees have left the brood-cells, by which time the early flowers will be withered? What is to be done in this dilemma? Mark the resources of the industrious bees. They search in the neighbourhood[I] for a place where they may deposit their honey, until the young shall have left the combs in which they were hatched. If they fail in this object, they crowd together in the front of their habitation, forming prodigious clusters. It is not uncommon to see them building combs on the outside."

[H] See 'The Bee-Preserver,' by Jonas de Gelieu, translated from the French; Edinburgh, 1829. This valuable little work contains the substance of sixty-four years' experience.

[I] The word here translated *neighbourhood* seems, with some, to have given rise to a misconception as to the meaning intended to be conveyed by it. From the context it is clear Gelieu only meant to imply some place of deposit in proximity to the parent hive, and not anything actually apart from it. He distinctly says, "provided there be an accessible way of communication between them." That bees do, in a degree, leave their usual domicile for the temporary storing of honey is evident, when from necessity they construct combs (often in the open air) on the underneath side of their floor; or work in a separate hive or box, placed against the original one.

In general, honey-gathering is altogether suspended, necessarily, under the circumstances we have stated; and, after a long course of inaction, in the very best part of the season, swarming follows. Indeed there always appears to be a connexion between swarming and idleness, induced by a succession of interregnums in the government, causing a suspension of breeding, when little or no store of any kind is collected. The proprietor must therefore make his election as to his course. If the multiplication of stocks is his object, his bees may thus be impelled to throw off swarms, but he must abandon the prospect of a large harvest of honey under such circumstances. This method of bee management is usually called *single hiving*, and is that commonly followed by cottagers, as on the whole the least expensive. On the general subject of swarming we shall enter more at large under the head of "Spring Management."

Depriving system.—Opposed to the mode of management in which swarming is systematically encouraged, is that whereby, under ordinary circumstances, it may be often prevented, and much valuable time, in the most productive part of the year, be rendered available for the purposes of adding to the wealth of the family. Let us observe the natural instinct of these little animals, and at the proper season provide them with such an occasional addition of storing-room as will enable them uninterruptedly to go on constructing fresh combs, to be filled with honey, unmixed with brood or other substances. This temporary receptacle, though in communication with the stock-hive, can at pleasure, in the way which will hereafter be described, be detached from it, without injury to the bees; these returning to their original habitation, in which the mother bee (although she may occasionally perambulate every part of her dominion,) ought exclusively to carry on the work of breeding. The honey obtained by this act of *Deprivation* is always supposed to be in excess of what is required for the wants of the family, and almost invariably pure in quality. Various have been the contrivances for effecting the separation of the storing and breeding departments in a hive. The bees, when pressed for room, will extend their operations almost in any direction, whether the accommodation is given above (which is termed *storifying*), at the bottom (*nadiring*), or *collaterally*. Equally indifferent are they to the material of the temporary receptacle. A second hive, box, or glass, placed over the stock, is termed a *duplet*, or more commonly a *super*; by which general name, as we proceed, any kind of storing vessel so placed will be designated. A productive season sometimes admits of a second super (usually introduced between the first and the stock), called in such case a *triplet*. An empty box or hive, pushed beneath a full one, is denominated a *Nadir*,—a mode of practice not always advisable except in the case of swarms of the same year, or towards the latter end of very abundant seasons. A still smaller addition to a common hive consists merely of a few bands of straw, on which it is raised temporarily, and this constitutes an *eke*. When either this or a nadir is used, and to facilitate its subsequent removal, a board ought to be placed between the stock-hive and the nadir, to prevent the combs from being worked down into it. The board may either be pierced with good-sized holes, throughout, or it may be cut into the form of parallel bars, as a grate, with about half an inch of space between them. The entrance to the stock-hive must be stopped, and one made at the bottom of the eke or nadir. We shall hereafter describe a modification of the Nadir principle, which, by way of distinction, I have called *Nethering*.

In contrasting, as we have done, the Swarming and Depriving systems, it should not be understood that either of them can invariably be advantageously carried out exclusively. An occasional change of system is desirable. In all large apiaries there is always a necessity for renewals both of Stocks and of Hives, by swarming; and it is seldom profitable, more especially as respects a common straw hive, to continue to work it on the depriving plan beyond a few seasons consecutively. Moreover, the cost of a new hive will be well repaid by an entire occasional renovation of the colony, stimulated thus to increased exertion, and with the advantage probably of a changed Queen.

The preference given to either of the two schemes of Bee management we have just detailed, must direct the proprietor in the choice of his hives, and we shall proceed to describe such of them as have found most favour among modern practitioners; premising that in using the term *Hive*, we intend its general acceptation, no matter of what material it is made. Neither is it our object unduly to magnify the advantages of wooden hives at the expense of those of straw: prejudice exists on both sides the question. They are each valuable according to circumstances, and their intended uses. Moreover, he only deceives himself and others who imagines he has discovered a system or a hive by which to command an abundance, or an improved quality of Honey, at pleasure. A favorable season may crown with success some cherished theory or mechanical device, to be followed in the next by disappointment; for he has little studied the natural habits of bees, who believes they can be made at will to conform, under all circumstances, to any settled scheme of practice we may devise for them. The attempt has led to the Babel of contrarieties too frequently exhibited amongst apiarian professors, to the confusion of the novice; each deprecating everything except the mode of procedure he has found applicable to his own case or district, and with which of course he is most familiar. In the words of Mr. Golding, "Let my readers repel the quackery which would have them believe that it was the *kind of hive* which commanded the honeyed store. No; that will be ruled by the productiveness of the season and the locality." Having taken the Honey bee under our especial protection, we are bound to provide for its due preservation from the effects of climate, &c., and perhaps, in addition to the ordinary attentions, the most that can be done with permanent advantage is to furnish our intelligent little workmen with a dwelling, convenient in its form and arrangement for the intended purposes; bearing in mind, as a general rule, that these are best consulted by an attention to simplicity in its details.

COMMON STRAW (OR SINGLE) HIVES.

In their wild state, bees have most usually found a secure residence in the decayed trunks of the thick forest trees. Where they are domesticated, the kinds and shapes, as well as the materials of bee-hives, vary according to climate and locality, or the purse of the proprietor. Those used in many parts of this country are made of straw, of a bell-shape, and being intended for single hiving, are usually without any means of enlargement. At the end of the second or third year, they are too often placed over the pit of destruction; and thus, with a little impure honey, flavoured with brimstone, the scene closes. Is it surprising that an unpleasant association is thus connected with the use of such hives? Happily for the cause of humanity, experience has decided that this consequence is not inevitable; and I trust I shall hereafter point out the method by which it may be avoided, and make it appear to be the interest of the proprietor *never to kill* his bees, let the hive be of what kind it may.

Common hives are best made of unthreshed rye, or good wheat straw. They would be much improved by a greater attention to shape, being usually too high in proportion to the width. It may be well, in this connexion, to introduce the observation of Gelieu. "One of my chief objects," says he, "has been to ascertain what shape of hive is the most profitable; and with this view I have tried all the different kinds, and have invariably remarked that bees thrive better in low hives than in high ones; that in general those which are broad and flat amass more honey, thrive better, and give out stronger and earlier swarms than those which are high. A hive thrives only in proportion to the success or perfection of its brood-comb in the spring. It is, therefore, of great importance to keep up the necessary degree of heat for the hatching of the brood. If, at that time, the bees are lodged in high and roomy hives, they will crowd together in vain, and the heat ascending is lost in the empty space above. This never happens in low flat hives, where it is more easily concentrated."

To prevent the combs from falling, sticks are commonly put across, or along the inside of a hive, as a support to them. But these props are an annoyance to the Bees, presenting difficulty in subsequently extracting the combs, and are never required in a hive made with a proper regard to proportion; in other words, where the combs are not too large to bear their own weight, when fully loaded. As regards the area of hives, much difference of opinion prevails, and a certain degree of latitude must be left for circumstances connected with locality, &c. Credit has been taken by some apiculturists, and doubtless with reason, for much reducing the unwieldy hives of our ancestors. On an average, perhaps, a preference may be given, as regards a common bell-formed straw hive, to one made about fourteen inches wide, and not more than eight inches high at the centre of the crown, both inside measure. There will be less of room wasted in a hive thus formed, inasmuch as the combs are stored down to the bottom cells, which is rarely the case in a high and narrow one. A low wooden hoop is often used, worked at the bottom of the hive; or, as Dr. Bevan says, "the lower round of straw may be begun upon a wooden hoop, the bottom of which has been planed smooth; it should be perforated through its whole course, and the perforations made in an oblique direction, so distant from each other as to cause all the stitches of the hive to range in a uniform manner." The hoop gives greater stability to the hive, preserves the lower edge from decay, and affords facility in moving it.

The custom of plastering round the bottom edge of a hive with mortar or clay is better omitted. Its own increasing weight will settle it down to its board: at all events no cement is equal to that used by the bees themselves; any other only serves to accelerate the decay of the hive, besides presenting an impediment on occasional removal for cleaning or inspection.

STRAW DEPRIVING HIVES.

A reference to the preceding section will show the reasons for giving a preference to rather shallow common straw hives over high ones, and the same arguments hold good where they are intended to be managed on the system usually termed of *Deprivation*; except that then the hive need be scarcely so large as in the case of single hiving. But to give facilities for the placing of a second hive, or super, over the original stock-hive, the latter ought to be made flat on the top, viz., cylindrical and straight in form. This shape found an advocate in the late Mr. Payne,[J] one of the most experienced instructors of Cottage Bee-keepers, who saw reasons for altering the dimensions of his hives from twelve inches wide to fourteen, and seven, or sometimes eight, inches in height (both inside measure), and which I have adopted as preferable.

In the centre of the crown of the hive is a three or four inch hole. The latter, when not in use, is stopped by a piece of worked straw, like a mat, as seen in the preceding illustration; and this may be fastened down by pins or a slight weight. At the proper time for placing a super, the straw mat cover can be removed, and its place supplied by what is termed an *adapter*, which is usually a piece of board the same diameter as the top of the hive, having a corresponding hole through its centre; thus in fact *adapting* it as the floor-board to a super. It will often be better, instead of one thick adapter, to have two very thin ones, of equal form and size, placed together. In such case, mahogany or some hard wood should be used, to prevent warping. On the removal of a full super, this double adapter will be found useful, as any impediment can be removed by passing between the two boards a knife, or some fine wire. Or a piece of tin, zinc, or thin wood may be inserted to entirely stop the communication, if desired, at any time.

[J] See the 'Bee-keeper's Guide,' by J. H. Payne.

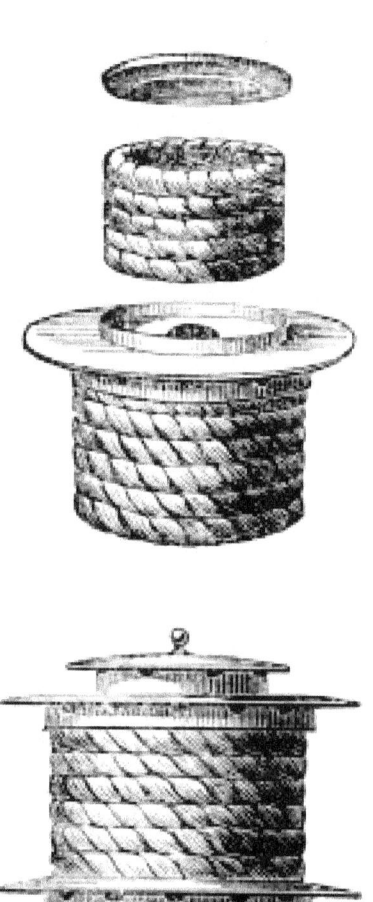

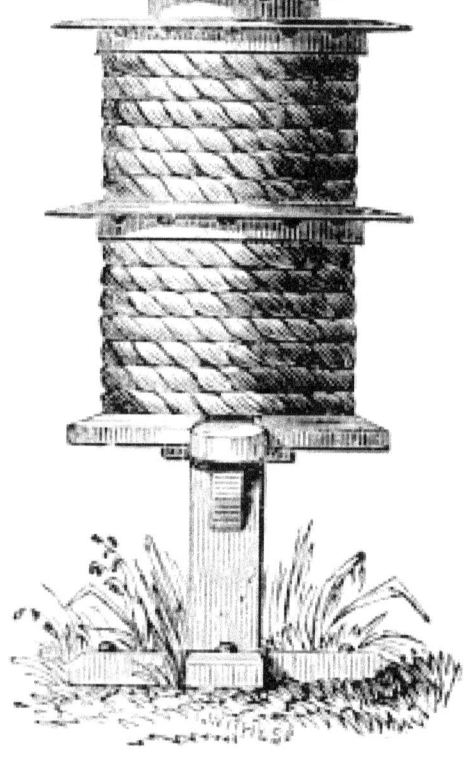

A straw super is best made of the same flat and cylindrical form as the stock-hive just described. The size may vary in diameter according to season and locality, from ten to twelve inches, or even the full width of the stock-hive, and three to six inches in inside height. In good years two or more of such supers may sometimes be filled in succession, the appearance of the hive determining its expediency. Should the stock-hive become hot and crowded before the first cap is entirely filled, a second smaller one (or triplet,) may be added. In such cases, the first super is always to remain the upper one, for it would be useless to put the triplet anywhere except *between* the two now in use, and it must have a two-inch hole in its crown as a passage upwards for the bees. In moving the first super, the upper half of the double adapter can be lifted with it, first introducing between them a piece of zinc or tin, to stop the communication with the stock-hive. In order to give the straw supers a better footing when placed one upon another, some persons prefer an extra cord or rim of straw to be worked round the outer bottom and top band. Or, if they are made plain, a thin hoop may be slipped round at the point of junction, embracing them both. A few holes are made in the hoop, for the reception of small pointed iron pins (easily removable), passing through and into the straw, and thus keeping it in its place. Those who choose may have the supers made without crowns, which gives facilities for fitting them up to serve any required purpose. This is done by means of loose wooden crown-boards: they may be prevented from warping by being made of two circular smooth boards glued together, the grain of the wood crossing. These boards are of different diameters; the smaller circle falls within the inner diameter of the cap; the other should be made an inch or more larger, to rest upon the upper edge of it. A reference to the engraving in the next page will illustrate our meaning. A small weight for a day or two will adjust the crown to its place; but any little apertures should in some way be stopped, for the escape of too much warmth must not be permitted. Mr. Golding does this by an effectual method: "Any little misfit," says he, "through which the bees may get out, is best stopped with a bit of tea lead, a store of which should be kept for such purposes." On removing a full cap, the combs can be separated from its sides with a knife or spatula, when there will be no difficulty in lifting up the crown-board with the combs suspended from it, in an unbroken state; and this often enhances their value.

Whether with or without the protection of a bee-house, the supers ought to be covered. For this object an exterior hive or straw cylinder may be used, similar in form and diameter to the stock-hive, and of any required height. The zinc shade and its cover, which will be more particularly described (under the head of hive-covers), suitably completes a protection of this kind. At present a reference to the preceding illustrations will suffice. The upper engraving shows a straw super with its moveable crown-board, and the method of placing it over a stock-hive; whilst the lower one represents the appearance of the whole when put together, with zinc shades and a cover.

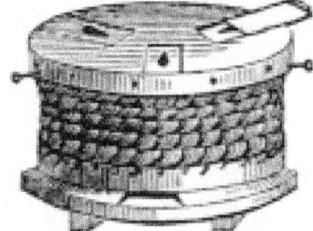

We have as yet supposed the stock-hive to be constructed in the usual way, with a flat straw crown; but many persons are induced to prefer wood; in which case the hive may be made in the mode pointed out for the caps, open at both ends alike. The same kind of moveable crown-board will in that case be suitable; made, as already detailed, of two circular pieces of wood of different diameters, together about three fourths of an inch in thickness. A little of some kind of luteing can, if needed, be used in adjusting the crown-board to its hive; or the tea lead we have just spoken of may often serve.

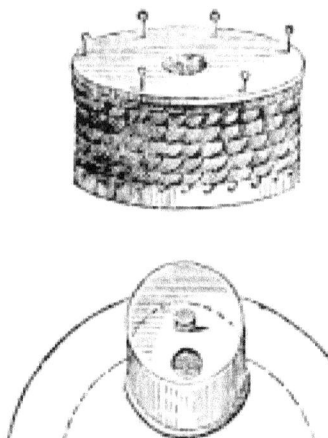

There is another mode of fitting a wood crown. This may be of the same size as the *outside* diameter of the hive, a thin hoop being screwed around its edge, with an inch additional; the whole fitting over as a cap. A few small pointed iron pins may pass through the lower edge of the hoop horizontally into the straw, thus sufficiently holding it; at the same time that its subsequent removal is easy. Instead of a hoop, I have used a strip of zinc, screwed round, and pinned, as just mentioned, which fits closer than wood, and when all is painted of one colour, has a neat appearance. Even without any kind of hoop, the wood top may be fixed by means of moveable pointed pins going through it, and down into the upper edge of the hive. Amateurs often prefer the crown-board cut with three holes, triangularly in position, to a single central one; as convenience is thus given for working three small glasses, or a large-sized one, as shown by the circles delineated in our illustration. The holes may be one and a quarter inch in diameter at the larger end, tapering two inches down to a point. Three zinc slides or *dividers*, as they are called, move in grooves, cut two inches wide from the edge of the crown-board, over the holes. The supers should be placed each on a separate adapter; and on removal, the slide is passed underneath the adapter, the whole being then lifted off together.

Various opinions have prevailed as to the expediency of painting the exterior of straw hives, some believing that absorption of vapour best takes place where it is omitted. My own idea is that, for exposed hives, an annual coat of paint is desirable, and nothing looks better for the purpose than a natural straw colour. We may resort to the words of Gelieu, who says, "it is commonly supposed that bees thrive best in straw hives, because the straw absorbs the moisture, and the combs are less liable to mould. For my part I can perceive no difference. The bees are careful enough to varnish over the interior of the straw hives with a coating of wax, or rather propolis, to prevent the settlement of the moths; and in the old hives this varnish is so thick that no moisture can penetrate between the cords of straw. Wooden hives will also absorb moisture to a certain extent; and experience has shown me that it is a matter of indifference which are employed, except as to the price."

HIVE-COVERS.

Whatever difference of opinion there may be as to the expediency of the practice of placing straw hives in the open air, independently of a house or shed, the custom prevails to so great an extent, that our object would be incomplete were we not to point out some of the modes resorted to for protecting them in such cases. Of the commoner kinds of coverings many are sufficiently unsightly; some being of straw thatch (or hackles), others of earthenware, in various ugly forms, and often objectionable and injurious to the hive, from their weight. In the apiary of a friend I have seen a dome-formed straw cover to a stock-hive, constructed with a projection all round of about three inches. On the underneath side are attached three or four bands in a circle, fitting over the outer diameter of the hive. The appearance of this cover is appropriate; but unless carefully painted, wet will eventually find admittance. It may, however, be rendered water-proof by means of some kind of cement. I have sometimes used for this purpose a mixture of paint with fine sawdust, pounded into the consistence of paste, and afterwards painted and varnished.

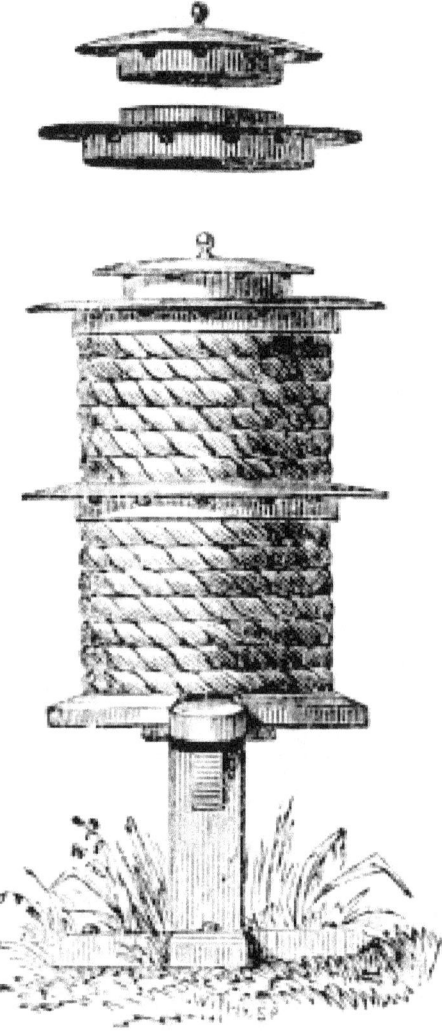

A cover of the same form can be manufactured in zinc, more or less convex, or sometimes nearly flat, its edges being turned down over stiff wire. A descending rim of not less than two inches deep is attached to the underneath side, encircling the upper edge of the hive. There ought to be perforations immediately under the projection of the rim, and a space left between the cover and the crown of the hive, for the passage of air; or a small worked mat, of straw bands, may be interposed to prevent any ill effect from a hot sun.

A modification of the last-described zinc cover I have used satisfactorily for the protecting of flat straw depriving hives, requiring more than one story in height. Immediately upon the stock-hive is introduced what, for want of a more distinctive term, I call a *shade*, encircling the upper edge, as just detailed, with the same kind of descending rim and air-holes. It is made of moderately thick sheet zinc, cut of such exterior diameter as to leave a projection round the outer edge of the hive of three to four inches, and turned a little downwards over stout wire, to throw off wet. In the centre of the shade is a circular opening, which, if required, may be of the same diameter as the interior of the stock-hive, and round it is a raised rim, standing up not less than half an inch. Within this central opening it is intended to place the super, of whatever kind it may be. A reference to what has been said at page 34, and the illustrations there given, as well as those now annexed, will show the construction of the shade; also the mode of covering the super by means of a second straw hive (made with or without a crown), standing upon the shade, the upright rim of which keeps it in its place. On the top of this upper hive a second shade, made like the first, may be placed. The completion of the whole is a slightly convex zinc cap, of about two inches in height, fitting securely over the central opening, like the top of a canister or pot. There is a projecting lateral rim to the cap, underneath which air-holes are made, similar to those under the projection of the shade. In winter, and at any time when a super hive is not required, the cap is placed over the shade immediately surmounting the stock-hive, reducing the edifice to one story. When feeding is needed by the bees, a pan may be introduced for the purpose within the central opening, and covered over by the zinc top. In reply to those who are dubious as to the expediency of using metal coverings, it may be remarked that no inconvenience arises in the present case, as neither the shade nor its cover come in contact immediately with the crown of the hive.

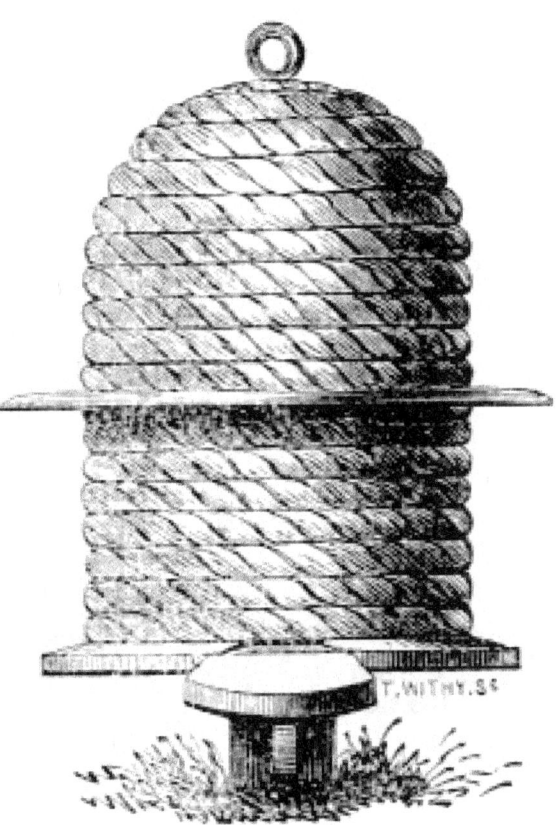

If a straw cover to a super is preferred, it can stand over the rim of the shade, as seen in the illustration annexed.

An effectual protection to a round hive may be made by means of an outer case, in fact merely a straw cylinder, with open ends. It must in diameter be large enough to drop loosely over the hive, and rest on the floor-board. The height ought to be sufficient to include any supers that may be required. Surmounting the whole, either one of the zinc covers, shown at page 39, of an enlarged size, can be used; or the shade and its top, as seen at page 40.

FLOOR OR HIVE-BOARDS.

The floor on which a hive is placed should be of wood, and not of any material too retentive either of heat or cold, as stone, slate, &c. In summer, the melting of the combs often results, and in winter, numerous lives are lost from chill. Every hive, of whatever kind, should stand upon its own separate board, so as to give facility for lifting, cleaning, or weighing the whole together at any time, without disturbance to the bees.

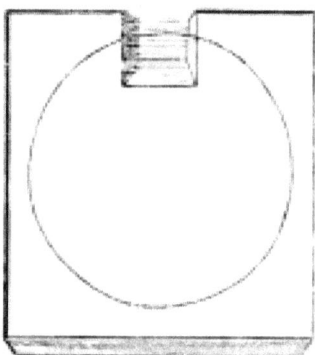

The entrance into a hive is generally cut out of its bottom edge. This has a tendency to cause decay in that part, particularly if of straw; besides that, a hole so made affords but indifferent protection from driving wet or a scorching sun, and gives imperfect facility for the escape of moisture from the hive. It is a better plan to sink the passage out of the thickness of the floor-board, till it reaches the inside of the hive. There are several ways of doing this, but a simple one is the following: Let the board be of thick, seasoned wood, and to prevent warping, screw two strong cross-bars to the underneath side, seven or eight inches apart. In size the floor-board ought to be a little larger than the exterior of the hive, from whence it should be chamfered down every way, to three eighths of an inch at the edge. From the latter, the entrance must be cut or grooved out, straight and level till it enters the inside of the hive, when it may slope upwards. This groove may be about four inches wide, and three eighths of an inch deep where the hive crosses it; for it is better in all instances that the requisite space at the door should be given laterally, rather than in height. This is not only more convenient to the bees, but shuts out from admission into the hive such guests as the snail or the mouse. In a board thus constructed a convenient mode of occasionally contracting the entrance-way is by means of small wooden blocks, of different widths, so formed that the lower half can be pushed within the hive's mouth. The board just described, and its blocks, are shown in the engraving beneath.

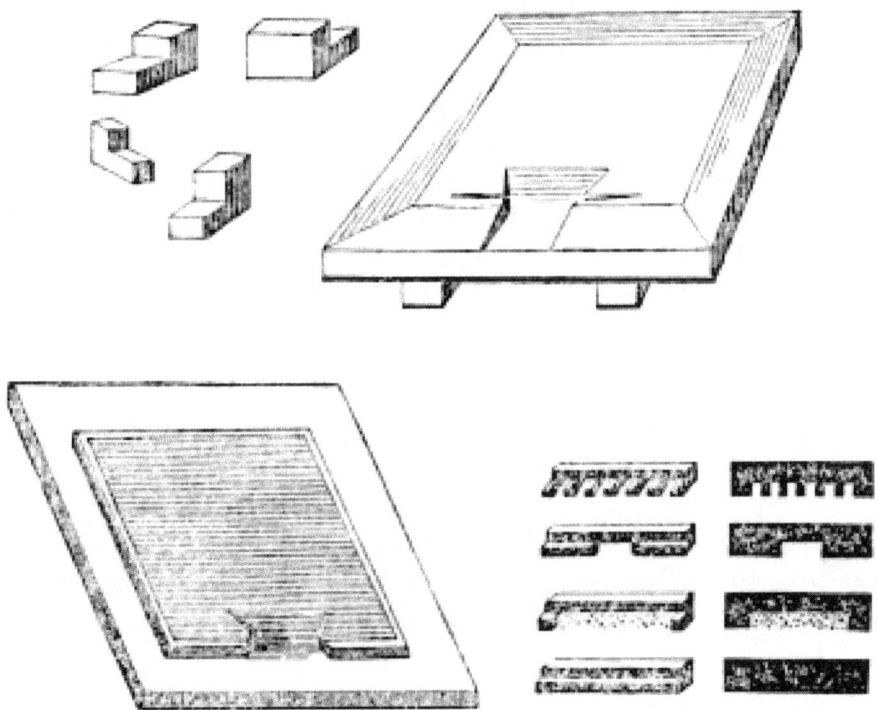

Another kind of hive-board, suitable for some description of boxes, is made by cutting a rabbet of any required width, and three-eighths of an inch deep, on all its sides, leaving the raised part of the board the size of the outside of the box, with an additional half inch beyond this, every way. The passage into the hive is to be cut from the edge of the rabbet, and on the same level, for about two inches; after which it must slope upwards. It may be four to five inches wide, and its sides should bevel a little outwards. This gives facilities for the introduction of moveable blocks or mouth-pieces, for the convenience of contracting or altogether stopping up the entrance, as may be required. The blocks are an inch wide, and must all be of one size, and of the same length and bevel as the entrance-way. In height they should be three quarters of an inch in front; cut down behind, half the width to three eighths of an inch. Thus made, the lowest half inch of the block is inserted within the mouth of the hive, and the other half projects on the outside. To suit all cases and seasons, blocks so formed may be cut on the lower part, from front to back, with any required passage-way through them at pleasure. The preceding engraving exhibits one of these boards, with a front and back view of four blocks thus varied; the third one being fitted with perforated zinc.

An entirely covered entrance, for those who desire it, is afforded by a double board, in which the passage is cut through the floor, altogether within the hive; and it may be thus made:

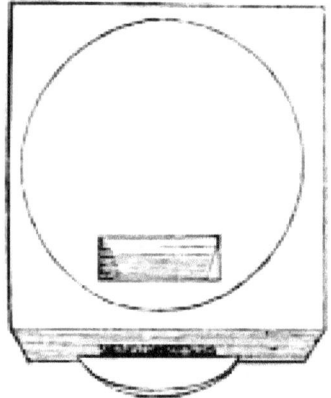

Take a piece of inch seasoned wood, an inch or two broader and longer than the hive. Smooth both sides, and underneath it cut a groove four or five inches wide, and four inches back from the edge. The part next the edge should be there hollowed out three eighths of an inch deep, increasing to double this at the other end, where it enters the hive. An opening through from the upper side must be made, to meet the underneath hollow, giving a gradual slope down into it. A piece of three-quarter inch board, seven to nine inches wide, must then be screwed underneath, the grain crossing the other; the doorway for the bees being of course between the two. The lower board should be a little the longest, the extra length being intended to form a small alighting board in front.

All the boards in the preceding illustrations are shown square as to form; but any of them may at pleasure be made round.

HIVE-STANDS, OR PEDESTALS.

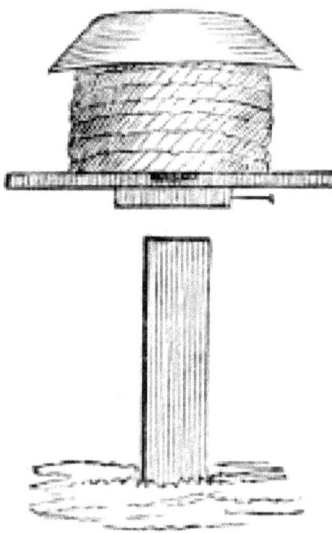

Hives standing singly, in the open air, must be so placed as that there is no risk of their being overthrown by the wind or other casualty, and various kinds of supports have been devised. Whatever is preferred, it ought to afford facilities for allowing the lifting up of the hive on its board at pleasure. A single pedestal or post is sometimes used, cut flat at the top to six or seven inches square. It may stand out of the ground fifteen or sixteen inches, and be firmly fixed, to avoid shaking, which alarms the bees. Sometimes a higher elevation than this is given, but it is not expedient to subject the hives unnecessarily to the action of the wind, any more than it is to place them so near the ground as to cause the bees to be affected by damp exhalations. On the underside of the centre of the hive-board fix four bars of wood (or three will do), of about two inches square, so as to form a cap or socket, fitting over the top of the pedestal. The board may be there secured by the insertion, diagonally, of one or two pins, through the sides of the cap and into the post. This plan may be varied by means of the two pieces or arms, let edgewise flush into the top of a post, crossing it diagonally: on this the hive-board may rest, or be secured by a button or two.

Or, on the top of a pedestal, four or five inches in diameter, a piece of board, of about nine inches square, may be fixed as a table. Upon this place the hive-board, of which the cross bars, appended to its underneath side, are so adjusted in point of distance apart, as to come on each side of the table, being there secured by a pin or turn-button.

This last-described stand may be improved, at a little further cost. Nail upon the pedestal a piece of strong board, eight or nine inches wide, and three inches longer than the outside width of the hive-board. Underneath the table thus formed, a couple of struts or angle-pieces must be fixed, to render the whole firm. The under-side bars of the hive-board are adjusted to fall on each side the table, as before detailed. The extra three inches of the latter must be thrown to the front, where it is designed to form a projecting alighting platform for the bees. This part is occupied by a piece of wood nailed to it, and chamfered to meet the hive-board, to which it forms a stay.

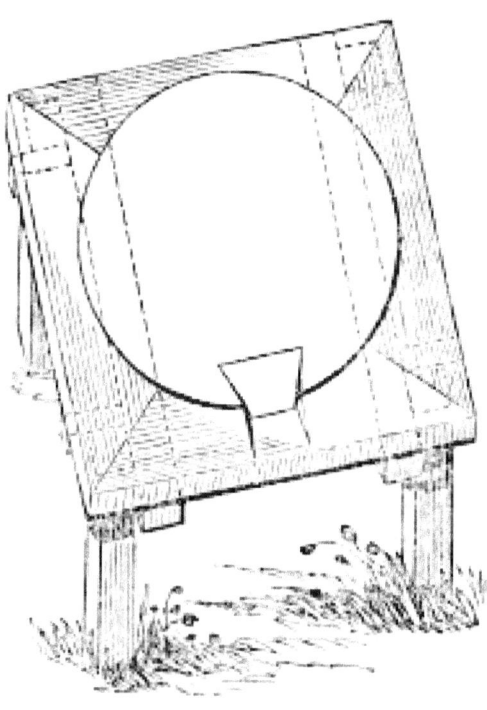

Another support to an out-door hive is made by means of four props, driven upright into the ground, and cut off level, at about sixteen inches high. The hive-board must have two cross bars screwed to its underside, from front to back, just coming within the uprights: to make it still more steady, four small blocks can be appended near the corners, between the cross bars and the edge of the board, to hold the latter in the opposite direction, as seen by the dotted lines in our illustration.

The same remark applies to the hive-stands just described as was made in the last section, viz., they can be adapted equally well to round as to square hive-boards. It may be well also to observe that, instead of sinking a pedestal into the earth, where decay soon ensues, it can be fixed upon strong cross pieces or feet, these being fastened to the ground by pins passing downwards through them.

Where there are a number of hives, instead of a separate stand for each, they may be placed more economically, and perhaps safely, on what I term a *hive-range*, of any required length. The range consists simply of a couple of rails, about an inch thick, and four inches in depth, nailed to the top outer edge of a series of posts, fixed firmly in or on the ground, about eighteen inches high. The space between the rails may be about twelve inches, measured withinside. The most suitable hive-board for a range is that shown at page 43. The cross bars on its underneath side must be so cut in point of length, as to fall within the two rails, where they are held; whilst what remains of the width of the board lodges upon them, with a convenient projection before and behind. Nor does it matter whether the hive-boards are made square or round. A range of this kind occupies very little space, and presents few facilities for the incursions of insects or other annoyers of bees. The hives ought to have a good interval between each; but it is an advantage that on this plan they can be moved, by sliding the boards to the right or left, if circumstances call for it. A range on the same principle might readily be made ornamentally, in part or wholly of iron, standing on feet, moveable anywhere, and setting vermin at defiance.

To the intelligent reader it is unnecessary again to repeat, that bee-stocks ought always to be raised sufficiently from the ground to protect them, not only from the baneful effects of damp, but from the incursions of vermin, &c. But inattention on this point is sometimes met with so gross, that we cannot forbear giving place to the preceding engraving, from a drawing made on the spot in Dorsetshire, illustrating the treatment to which the poor bees may be sometimes subjected by indifference or deplorable ignorance.

WOODEN BOX HIVES.

As far as we have proceeded, our attention has been directed principally to Straw hives. Those, however, of Wood have in modern times come pretty generally into use, when cost is not an object, as being more durable, less liable to harbour vermin, and better adapted, from their square form, for a convenient arrangement of the combs, besides admitting of glass windows.

As regards the plainer kind of boxes, either intended for use on the swarming system, or on that where deprivation is practised, I adhere to the opinion expressed as to straw hives, and prefer those constructed broad and shallow to such as are high and narrow. They may be made of the lighter and more porous kinds of deal, some preferring red cedar; but whichever is made use of, it should be thoroughly seasoned, and well put together; observing that the grain of the wood always runs in the horizontal direction, when its tendency to expansion or contraction is rendered of no importance. Conflicting opinions prevail as to the best size for bee-boxes; but, like almost everything else where these insects are concerned, something must be left dependent on circumstances and locality, as well as the intended mode of working them. A fair average size for a plain box is eleven and a half inches square, by eight inches deep, withinside; or, perhaps better, twelve by seven or seven and a half inches, clear; the thickness of wood throughout being not less than an inch, or, if exposed, more than this. The cover of the box should have a small projection on all sides, for better appearance, and to afford convenience for lifting. On the top a two- or three-inch hole may be cut in the centre, for the purposes of supering, of feeding, or ventilation. Instead, however, of one central hole, some persons like to have three smaller ones, cut triangularly; affording convenience for the use of a single large, or three small glasses. It is best to leave the roof of the box, withinside, unplaned, as the bees have sometimes a difficulty in making the first combs adhere to too smooth a surface. A window may be placed at the back, and another at one side, about four inches high, and six wide. The glass should be thick, and secured by putty; but it must not fit too tightly, or it is apt to crack from the swelling of the wood. There are various ways of covering the windows, but the best is, perhaps, by a sliding shutter of zinc. Round the window there must be a projecting moulding, mitred at the corners. On one side the piece of moulding is moveable, and to the back of this is screwed a plate of sheet zinc. This passes into a rabbet to receive it, cut, on the remaining three sides, at the back of the lower edge of the moulding. Where uniformity of appearance is studied, blank windows may be made opposite to the real ones.[K] No entrance-way should be cut in the box, as this more properly belongs to the floor-board.

[K] As regards windows, they are always useful to inspect a hive, but should, as a rule, be kept darkened. At the same time there is no doubt that bees will work exposed to the light, when the option of darkness is not allowed them. A friend put a swarm into a unicomb hive, made without shutters on each side, and exposed to the full glare of light at a window, which I frequently inspected. The bees filled the hive in a short time, paying apparently no attention to the eyes often observing their operations. It is to be remarked, however, that whether bees are in light or darkness, the one or the other must be continuous, as alternations disturb and alarm them. We shall hereafter give a design for an experimental *Light Hive*.

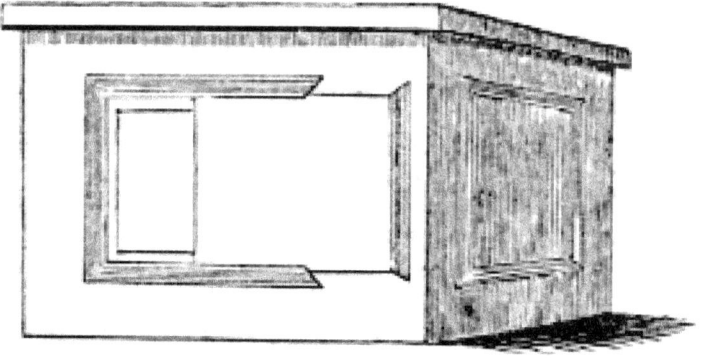

A reference to the engraving will show a box thus made, with its sliding shutter. It ought to be painted a sufficient time before use, or the smell is offensive to the bees; indeed, I have known a swarm forsake a box in consequence. I may observe, however, that some persons prefer boxes, when in a house, to be unpainted. They are always best placed under some kind of cover, as protection from wet and a hot sun is necessary to prevent warping and splitting, and not unfrequently the melting of the combs. Some German bee-keepers have recommended box-hives made long from back to front, and narrow from side to side.

WOODEN BAR BOXES.

An undoubted improvement on the box described in the last section, consists in the addition of separate moveable bars of wood, crossing the top of the hive, in parallel lines, to which the combs are to be attached. By this means any comb, on removal of the cover, can be separately extracted, adhering to its own particular bar. The *bar-system*, as we may call it, has had many advocates, but to none are we more indebted than to Dr. Bevan and Mr. Golding, for reducing to fixed rules what had previously been undefined and uncertain. The latter, however, appears to have a preference for straw hives, and has given instructions for adapting bars to them. We shall hereafter describe a hive of this kind, but varying in some respects from Mr. Golding's. With Dr. Bevan, many prefer boxes; and a square form is better than any other, as in these every bar has the advantage of being alike, fitting anywhere, either in the same or another box. At all events, "whatever the construction of the hive," says Mr. Golding, "without some such facility as bars, whereby every comb can be made individually available, there is something wanted, something wrong." With no claim, therefore, to the invention of any new principle, the boxes I have constructed are modifications of those that preceded them; the object in view being to render these, at a small extra cost, more manageable to the amateur. In short, I know of no hive more completely under control.

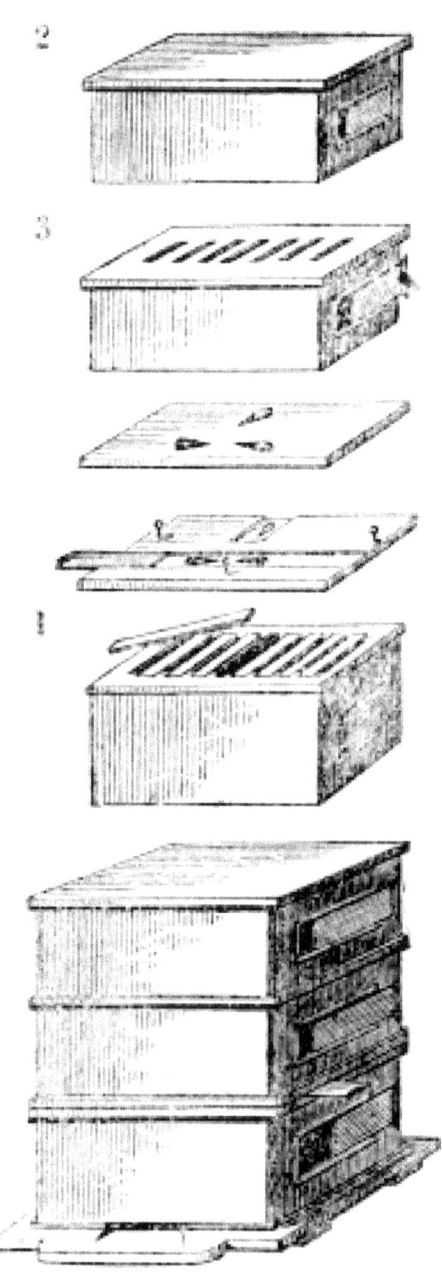

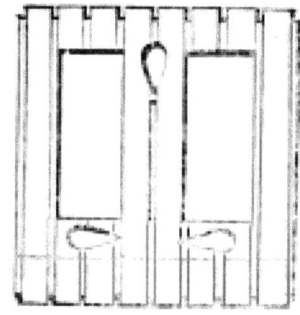

I may premise that the boxes (as illustrated in a former edition), following those described by Dr. Bevan, were adapted for the reception of seven bars. Subsequent experience has shown that these may be advantageously increased to eight in number, extending the square of the hive, but diminishing its height. In thickness the wood ought not to be less than a full inch. The dimensions withinside are thirteen and a quarter inches square; the height being seven inches, inclusive of the bars. As regards windows, there may be one at the back and at the side, four inches high by seven or eight inches long; with sliding shutters, like those described in the preceding section. The glass ought to be so fixed as to leave as little recess as possible withinside the box, otherwise the extraction of the combs is impeded. Indeed, it is better to have the panes introduced flush, and cemented from the inner side into a fine rabbet. The best kind of cement for this purpose is a mixture of powdered chalk and glue. The bars must be one and an eighth inch wide, and half an inch thick; being best unplaned on the underside, to enable the combs to adhere to them. Recesses of a full eighth of an inch are cut from the upper inner edge of the box, to receive the ends of the bars, into which they should fall easily, ranged from front to back. It is essential to follow the rules laid down by Dr. Bevan, who says, "if the distances of the bars from each other be nicely adjusted, there will be interspaces between them of about half an inch. The *precise* width of the bars should be attended to, and also their distances from each other, as any deviation in this respect would throw the combs wrong. It is better to be somewhat *within* the rule than to exceed it by ever so little, for the tendency is generally to make the combs approximate. This has induced me to vary a little the relative distances of the bars, the three (four) centre ones being placed only seven sixteenths of an inch from each other, whilst the rest gradually recede from that distance." For the purpose of ensuring the needful uniformity and correctness of workmanship requisite in all points, I constructed a pattern gauge, as seen in the annexed engraving. It is made of sheet metal, brass being the best, of the same dimensions as the interior square of the boxes, exclusive of the end projections. These latter denote the exact interspaces between the bars; so that if the gauge is placed upon the inner edge of the box, the position of the recesses into which the bars are intended to fall may be indicated at each end. Moreover, the gauge gives a correct pattern for making the bars, as also the position of the holes through the crown and centre boards.

It may be well here to allude to what some have thought to be an improvement in the construction of the bars, the object being to render the combs more accessible, and the usual cutting, to detach them from the sides of the hive, avoided. A reference to the accompanying engraving will exhibit a bar with a frame suspended beneath it, but so made as not to touch either the sides or bottom of the hive, and within which the combs are, or ought to be, wrought. Doubtless, advantages may arise from the facilities thus given for removal, provided these are not counterbalanced by the evil of greater complication, and the inconvenience arising from the possible attachment by the bees of the frame itself to the sides of the hive, and so setting them fast. Moreover, as such frames curtail space in the hive, allowance is necessary in its external dimensions.

A cover or crown board, three quarters of an inch thick, clamped at the ends, and projecting all round nearly half an inch, is fixed down, flush with the bars, with two or three long screws. To prevent rusting, these may be of brass.

Some objection has been raised against screws, as being occasionally troublesome to remove. The engravings annexed (drawn half size) show another mode of attaching the crown board by means of brass rings, elongated like the link of a chain, and held loosely at the bottom by the head of a screw, inserted at the side of the box. An aperture is cut in the projection of the crown board, through which the link passes to the top, into a recess made to receive it, and where it is fixed by a moveable lateral pin, leaving a flush surface. On removing the pin the link drops down upon the screw head, and the crown board becomes released. Instead of a ring, a similarly formed link can be cut from a piece of sheet metal.

It is not always that amateurs are possessed of the nerve requisite to perform, periodically, the operation of changing the cover immediately over a populous stock. The construction of my bar-hive renders this unnecessary. Through the cover are three openings, cut as a passage upward for the bees into a super. For convenience, two of these are placed within three inches of the front of the box (measuring inside), to the centre of the holes, which are one inch and a quarter in diameter at the outer end, lengthening towards the centre to three inches; there diminished to a point, and leaving two intermediate inches between them. I have found it well in this part to give an increased facility to the bees in passing over the bars, which otherwise too much intercept the passage. To accomplish this, let the crown board be turned bottom upwards, grooving out the central portion coming immediately underneath and between the two holes, for the space of six or seven inches long, one and a half inch wide, and three eighths of an inch deep. The third hole is made an inch and a half from the back of the cover (measured inside); of the same size and form as the others, but an inch shorter. This will be useful in working glasses and in feeding. The elongated form given to the holes is best adapted to prevent killing or maiming the bees in introducing the dividing slides. The latter are plates of stout zinc or copper, two inches wide, sliding within a recess or groove, cut their own thickness, across the top of the crown board, over the holes. The slides are long enough to meet in the centre, their outer ends being a little turned up for convenience. If the last inch is perforated with small holes, the slide becomes a ventilator, by drawing it out a little.

This hive may be used either for single or double hiving, or with any kind of super; but to render it complete for all purposes, there ought to be three boxes, forming a set, as seen in the engravings at p. 56, in which the stock-box is the bottom one. In many seasons and localities, however, the third box might not be called for. For convenience of description, the numbers 1, 2, and 3, are used in reference to the *stock-box*, the *first super*, and the *centre box*; all to be of equal size as to the square. No. 2 should be fitted with bars and windows, like the first; but in height it may be one inch, or sometimes two, lower. Moreover, there must be no holes through its crown board, for whether two or three boxes are in use, No. 2 is always the upper one. A great convenience is given by the introduction of a loose centre board, placed on the top of the stock-box, and of the same dimensions; being in fact an adapter to the super, which can be lifted upon it, on removal. It is of half-inch wood, clamped, having openings cut through, corresponding in form and position with those of the stock-box, but without any recess. The slides move beneath the centre board, opening or shutting off the communication from box to box, as required. No. 3 box differs from the others in being still shallower, and having no moveable bars. Moreover, the central portion of its cover is cut through into the semblance of a grating, as shown in the illustration, with six bars, nine inches long, of an inch and an eighth in width, and with interspaces of half an inch. In certain very productive seasons, and when the super No. 2 is filled, No. 3 may be introduced *between* the two others; not removing the upper box till the bees have commenced working in No. 3. A temporary close cover must then be placed over the grated one of the latter. Many experienced apiarians, however, object to using more than one super hive, preferring to give any further room that may be required, at the *bottom* of the stock. The box No. 3 is equally well adapted for either alternative; for it may go as a nadir, beneath the stock-hive, taking its place on the hive-board, in which latter is the entrance for the bees, no other being permitted.

A hive-board suitable is either like the one shown at p. 43, or that at p. 44; the boxes being placed upon it, with the bars ranging from front to back. Some persons are inclined, instead of one central entrance to the stock-box, to prefer two smaller ones, placed respectively at the outer extremities of the front, of course cut from the floor board; and it is probable that this departure from the general practice may not be without its occasional advantage, in winter especially, in a broad, shallow hive.

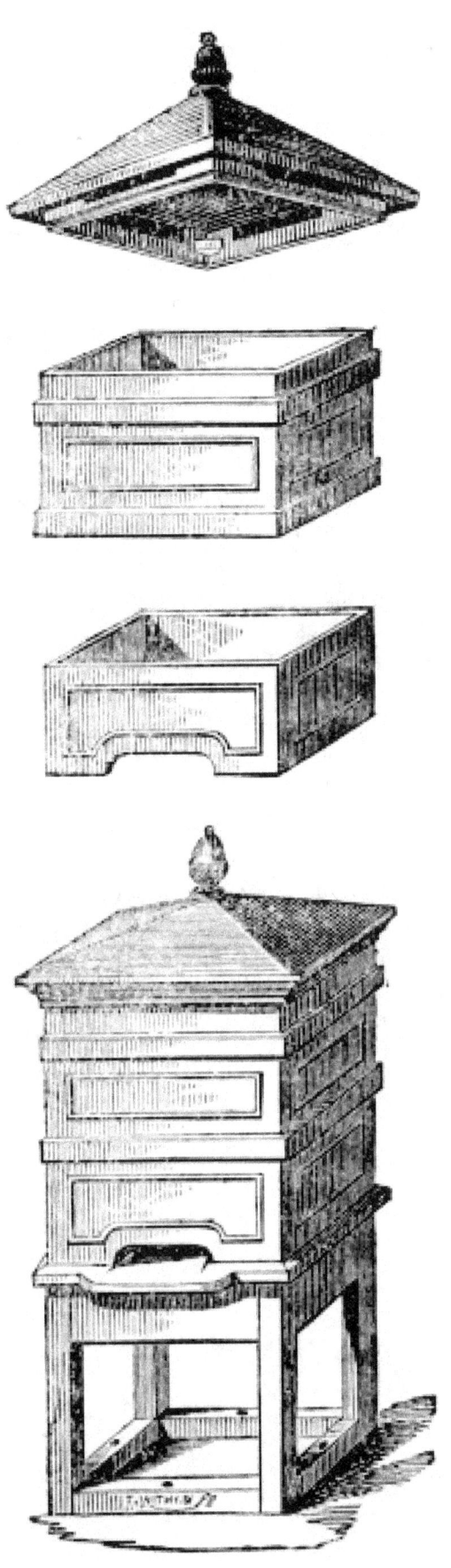

These boxes, like all wooden hives, should be placed in a house of some kind, if possible; but instances occur where such a convenience is not available. To meet these, I will describe a substitute, which gives effectual protection, though it would still be better standing under a shed. A recurrence to the engraving in the next page will show that our plan comprises an outer casing, in two compartments, and surmounted by a top cover or roof. They may be of half-inch wood, large enough in the square to drop loosely over the boxes, the lower compartment resting upon the rabbet of the hive-board, which may be made as shown at page 44, and wide enough to leave, on three sides, an outside margin of an inch. On the front side a rather more extended margin may be expedient. The height of the lower compartment, measuring from the rabbet of the floor board, reaches to the top of the stock-box, except just as much as will allow the slides to pass over its edge. A good-sized elliptical opening faces the mouth of the hive; or increased to two, where there is a second entrance. The other compartment of the case should be high enough to enclose within it the two upper boxes. To its outer bottom edge, a band or fillet, about two inches wide, and nearly half an inch thick, is appended, half its width. The other half-width is intended to overlap the outer upper edge of the lower case, when placed one upon the other; and this part should be chamfered, so as to go on and off easily. For appearance' sake, another band is appended to the upper case, near its top; unless any other exterior architectural embellishment is preferred. A reference to the engraving will show the whole design is completed by a hipped roof or cover. Under the four projecting edges of the latter is a suspended cornice, about two inches deep, on its outer sides. When in its place, about three quarters of an inch of the cornice ought to overhang, dropping loosely over the upper outer edge of the case (a little chamfered); to regulate this, recessed at the four angles, within the cover, are attached cross corner blocks. For the purpose of ventilating the roof, long lateral openings are cut out on the four sides, from the upper part of the cornice, under the projecting edges of the roof. The total projection of this may be two inches, or a little more. The cover ought to fit equally well upon either compartment of the case; for in winter the edifice can be reduced to one story only.

The stand for the whole is simply an open frame, of the same outside dimensions as the cases; with inch-thick rails, four inches deep, framed at the corners to four posts or legs. These may be two inches square, and eighteen inches high; either sunk into the ground, or placed upon it, by means of cross-pieces, pinned or pegged down. The hive-board drops loosely down into the frame, and rests upon the rails, showing a projection all round of an inch; the cross bars on its underneath side retaining it steadily.

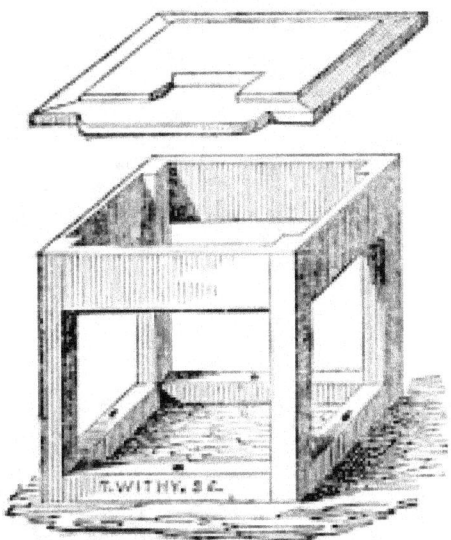

In a former edition, this kind of hive, when thus fitted up with an outer covering, obtained the name of the *double* bar-hive, by way of distinction from another mode of constructing it, which will now be detailed.

Whatever may be said about the inexpediency of placing wooden hives in exposure to the weather, the one we are now proceeding to describe was intended to meet the wishes of some bee-proprietors, who objected to the small degree of trouble, involved in using any kind of outer casing; obtaining from this circumstance the appellation of the *single* bar-hive.

The three boxes, forming the set, differ but little from those last described; the interior dimensions, bars, windows, crown-boards, &c., being similar; but the centre board is omitted, and the thickness of the wood must be increased to not less than one and a quarter inch. A rabbet of a quarter of an inch is cut round all the crown-boards, to receive a super box, or the roof cover; the better to retain it in its place. The outside projection should be extended to not less than an inch and a half; this part being chamfered to throw off wet. The plan of the roof cover will be seen on reference to our illustration. The square appended within it is in interior diameter the same as the boxes, to fit over any of them, resting upon it sufficiently to allow the projecting parts of the crown-board to be seen as a cornice. Beyond this, there is a further projection of the roof of an inch, provision for ventilation being made by a double set of openings, cut as shown in our engraving. For better security in winter, loose wooden blocks, to the stock-box, may be made to fill the space intervening between the glass windows and the sliding shutters. The hive-board may be that shown either at p. 43, or 44, of the same dimensions as that of the crown-boards, and chamfered off. The stand to receive it is like the one described and shown at p. 66, the square of its frame being the same as that of the exterior of the boxes. Our engraving exhibits a simple method of adding a useful kind of porch to the entrance of the stock-box, by means of a strip of zinc or other material, of the width of the front projection of the floor board. It can be bent into the form of an elliptical arch, the two lower extremities being held by going down within the sunken part of the board, whilst the upper part derives support by being pressed back beneath the window moulding.

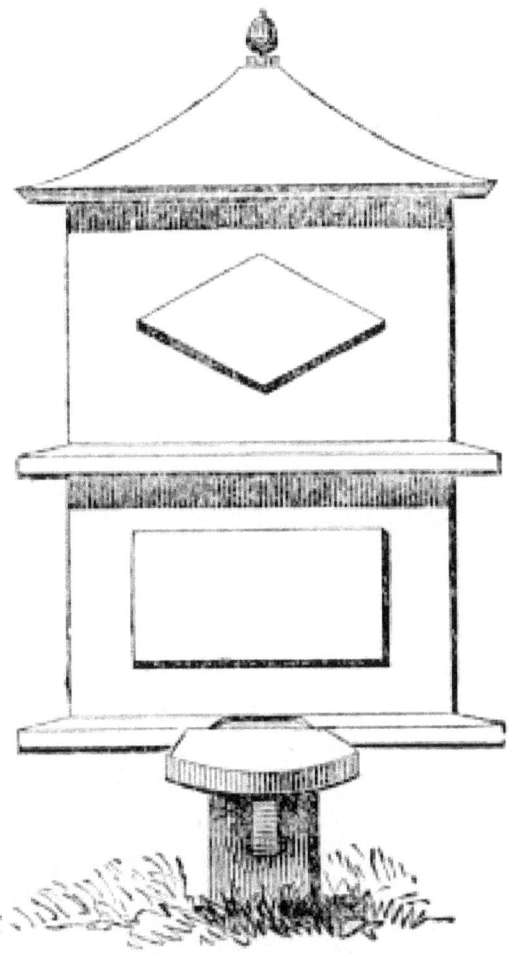

Those who study economy may, instead of the entire set of boxes just described, retain the stock-box only, with a cover to receive any kind of super, as shown above. The cover will do if made of half-inch wood, nine inches high to the square of the roof; the outside dimensions being the same as in the stock-box. A slanting projecting roof forms a part of the cover. Under its projecting edges openings for ventilation can be cut. The cover is retained in its place by a rabbet cut round the top of the stock-box, and preventing the admission of wet.

The object of the bars we have said is to furnish parallel foundations on which the combs are to be worked, for without an observance of this regularity, subsequent extraction becomes impossible; showing the necessity for a proper *beginning*. To induce the bees to preserve a straight direction, it has usually been found expedient to append what are termed *guide-combs* to three or four of the centre bars of the stock-box, previously to hiving a swarm into it; and for the purpose some pieces of clean *worker-comb* ought to be kept in reserve. In giving the needful directions for fixing the guides, we cannot do better than use the words of Mr. Golding, who says, "this is easily effected by heating a common flat-iron, slightly warming the bars with it, then melting a little bees'-wax upon it. The comb is now drawn quickly across the heated iron, and held down upon the centre of the bar, to which it firmly adheres, if properly managed. These pieces of guide-comb need not be more than two or three inches in diameter. Care should be taken that the pitch or inclination of the cells is upwards from the centre of each comb." Or it may do equally well, if the edge of the comb is dipped in melted wax.

In the absence of guide-combs another mode of proceeding has been sometimes successfully resorted to. Take a flat piece of tin or zinc (or stiff paper might do), of the length and width of one of the bars: cut out the central portion to the extent of half an inch in width. Lay the pattern thus prepared upon the bar, and with a brush smear, in a straight line, some melted bees'-wax along the central half-inch opening, and so proceed with four or five other bars. The bees will usually commence working first upon the waxed part of the bar, and this tends to uniformity subsequently. Nothing can be more beautiful than a box of honey-combs thus regularly worked; nor is it possible in any other way to have them so perfect and unbroken, when detached. Indeed, the convenience of moveable bars can only be appreciated by those accustomed to their use. Their advantage is apparent when it has become expedient to remove old combs from stock-hives. They may be made available in cases where one box has more and another less of sufficient store of honey: in such event, or as a substitute for feeding, a loaded bar or two can be transferred from the one to the other; or from a super to a stock-box. For the object of making artificial swarms great facility is given, more especially when a comb contains a royal cell. A brood-comb may in like manner be taken and inserted in a weak stock, to strengthen the population; or for the purpose of rearing a Queen artificially, in a hive wanting one. So also, in the swarming season, supernumerary royal cells may be cut out: likewise, a superabundance of drone-combs can be removed, and the bees will fill the vacancies with common ones.

We shall, under the head of *Autumnal management*, give general directions for the removal or deprivation of full super boxes; but it may be well here to describe the method to be pursued where it is necessary to operate on a *stock-hive*. In such a case, a piece of board is useful, of the same width and thickness as the top, or crown-board. In the middle of the day, unscrew the latter, sliding it sideways; the extra board covering over the vacancy as you proceed. In this way, only as much space as is wanted to get at any given bar need be exposed. "A few puffs of smoke," says Mr. Golding, "may now be blown down the sides of the comb to be taken out, which will intimidate the bees, and drive them away. A double-edged knife-blade, an inch and a half long, and three eighths of an inch wide, turned at right angles from the end of an iron rod of about a foot in length, is now passed down the edges of the comb, to detach them from the hive. After this is done, the comb may be easily lifted; such bees as still adhere to it being swept down into the hive as the bar is lifted upwards. Such operations as these are much less formidable than many persons believe. The fact is, the bees, when once intimidated by the smoke, may be done almost anything with. Quietness and a little tact are all that is required. When combs are taken out, they may be either detached from the bars at once, and the bars returned, or spare bars may be kept on hand wherewith to replace such as have been extracted."

BAR GLASS-HIVE.

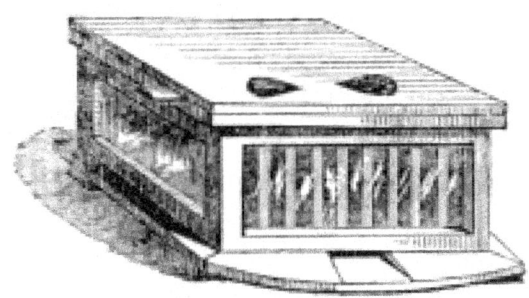

Before we leave the subject of box-hives, it may be interesting to give a description of one recently constructed by me for experimental purposes, as referred to in the note at page 53, and here illustrated. It may not improperly be termed a *Light*, or *Observatory Hive*, in distinction from the usual mode of rendering the dwelling as dark as possible. The hive itself resembles the bar-boxes just described, as to its interior dimensions, bars, crown-board, &c.; but differs inasmuch as it is made simply as a frame, filled in on the four sides with thick glass, flush with the inside surface of the wood. For the purpose of preventing the bees from attaching the combs to the glass, thin upright strips of wood, rather more than half an inch wide, are tacked under the centre of each bar, at both ends, extending from top to bottom inside of the hive. Or some might prefer to use frame-bars, like the one described and illustrated at page 58; but guides or waxed bars must be used, to ensure the regularity of the combs, and prevent an obstruction to the sight. The hive ought to be placed in a house, and in winter should be carefully covered; an outer case or box going over all.

STRAW BAR-HIVE.

We have already alluded to hives of straw, fitted with bars. The one now about to be described differs from those commonly used, in several respects, as will be seen on reference to the annexed illustration.

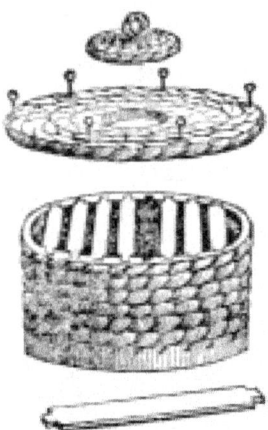

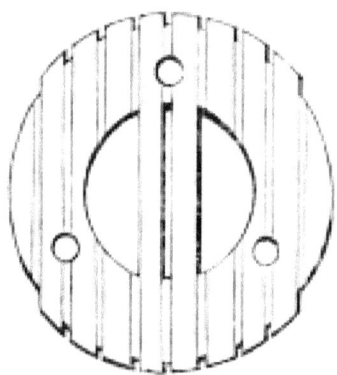

In form, my hive is an open cylinder, 14 inches in inside diameter, and 7 inches in height, to the upper side of the bars, which are eight in number; similar in size, and interspaced like those in the square bar-hive, described at page 56. For the purpose of supporting the bars, a well-seasoned hoop is introduced within, and on a level with, the upper edge of the hive—nearly two inches in depth, and a quarter inch thick; its interior diameter being the same as that of the hive. The two upper straw bands of the latter are reduced in size, sufficiently to form a recess equal to the thickness of the hoop,—the outside of the hive remaining flush. The hoop is there retained by a few small brad-nails, driven through it and into the straw; and thus no impediment is offered on extracting the combs. A difficulty presented itself in attaching the bars to the edge of the hoop, to overcome which I constructed a pattern-gauge, differing in form from that seen at page 57. Our illustration will show that the outer edges of the gauge are divided, so as, when laid flat upon the hoop, to give the precise position of the indentations for the reception of the ends of the bars: moreover, these may severally be correctly fashioned by following the form shown upon the gauge. The adjustment of the bars should be done previously to attaching the hoop to the hive, not allowing them to fit too tight. The cover is a flat piece of worked straw, which ought to lie *close* upon the bars. I have found no better method of securing the cover in its place than by the use of a few pointed iron pins, going down through it and into the upper edge of the hive. For convenience of working supers, a three-inch hole is left in the centre of the cover; stopped, when not in use, by a small piece of worked straw, pinned down. Some persons might prefer a wooden top, which may be perforated either with one hole or three. It should rest upon the bars, and can be held in its place by pins, in the way we have just mentioned, and which at any time are removable; or a hoop may be attached to the edge of the crown-board, as described and shown at page 35.

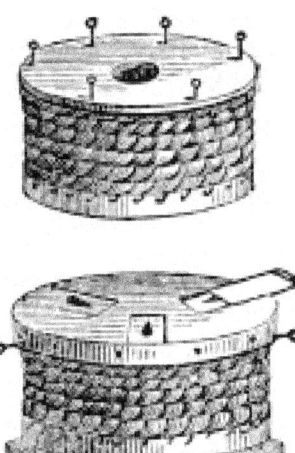

CIRCULAR WOODEN HIVES.

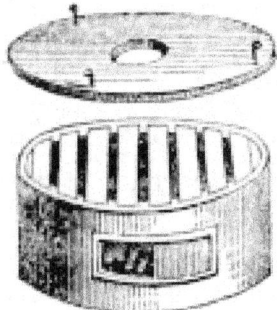

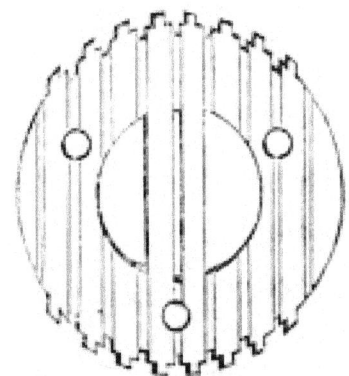

I have sometimes turned my attention to cylinders of wood, as offering great advantages in constructing a hive; not only in attaching bars, but also the desirable convenience of windows. The facilities for procuring them made with the requisite correctness of form, however, depends on circumstances not always at command; the process of construction being the same of steaming, rolling, and shaping, employed by the manufacturers of our common wooden corn measures, &c. The cost of the wood cylinders alone are not much more than the straw ones, and being made of oak or ash, they are very durable. Softer and more porous wood would doubtless be preferable, but a difficulty attends the use of such. In size, the dimensions before recommended are adhered to; viz., 14 inches clear, by seven inches in height, for hives with or without bars; the thickness being about half an inch. A reference to our illustration, and to the accompanying pattern gauge, will show the mode of cutting and adjusting the bars; these resting rather loosely in rabbets, cut the width of the bar, half through the thickness of the hive. The crown-board may be made and cut in the way already described, and can be fixed by means of a few small screws; or, if preferred, in the method detailed and illustrated at page 59. When the hive is not fitted with bars, it is an advantage partially to sink the crown-board within the diameter of the cylinder, which ensures a more perfect joint. At the back is a window of bent glass, protected by a sliding zinc shutter, moving in a frame of rabbeted moulding; all following the curved form of the wood. A suitable staining and varnishing gives to the whole a neat appearance. Two of the hives may be placed one upon the other, for supering; an adapter or centre board going between them: or smaller wooden round hives, of any size, with thin tops, can be used for the same purpose; and these might be made by a common cooper.

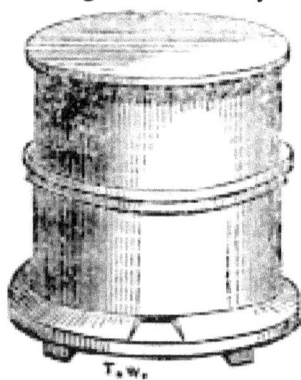

These hives are of too recent introduction to warrant saying more than that, to adapt them to the object in view, it is essential that they be placed in a house or cover, as from the density of the wood they are not calculated to bear exposure to the sun and weather. In winter attention should be given to close covering them. I may add that, in using a thinner cylinder, I have tried the experiment of coating the outside with an envelope of *gutta percha*, giving the advantage of improved appearance, and doubtless of utility, but at a considerable increase of cost.

COLLATERAL SYSTEM.

Various modes of working hives collaterally, or side by side, have been devised, but a very simple one has been practised with success by a correspondent, which as adapted by me may with propriety be termed a *doubling-board*. It is formed of a plain board not less than an inch thick. It must be of sufficient width to take a broad shallow hive, and long enough to contain two of these, with six or eight inches to spare. A stock-hive is in the first instance placed over the centre circular mark, within which is the double outlet for the bees. When more space is required, it must be moved over one of the side circles, and a second hive placed over the other. The double outlet forms a communication within the floor-board from hive to hive. The part hollowed out for this purpose is five inches wide, six inches long, and half an inch high inside, a sloping way being cut on the two further sides down into it. Two covered passages lead from this, terminating at one point on the alighting-board. The bees, having been accustomed to both these passages, will commonly take to the second hive, and commence working therein, particularly if smeared with honey. In order to show the position of the parts hollowed out, these are slightly shaded in the engraving. They are cut from the bottom side of the board, in the way described at page 45. A second piece of wood, nine or ten inches wide, must be screwed to the underside, to enclose the openings. This ought to reach back nearly the width of the upper board; at the same time projecting far enough in front to form the alighting-place. Another cross piece may be screwed to the underside, at each end.

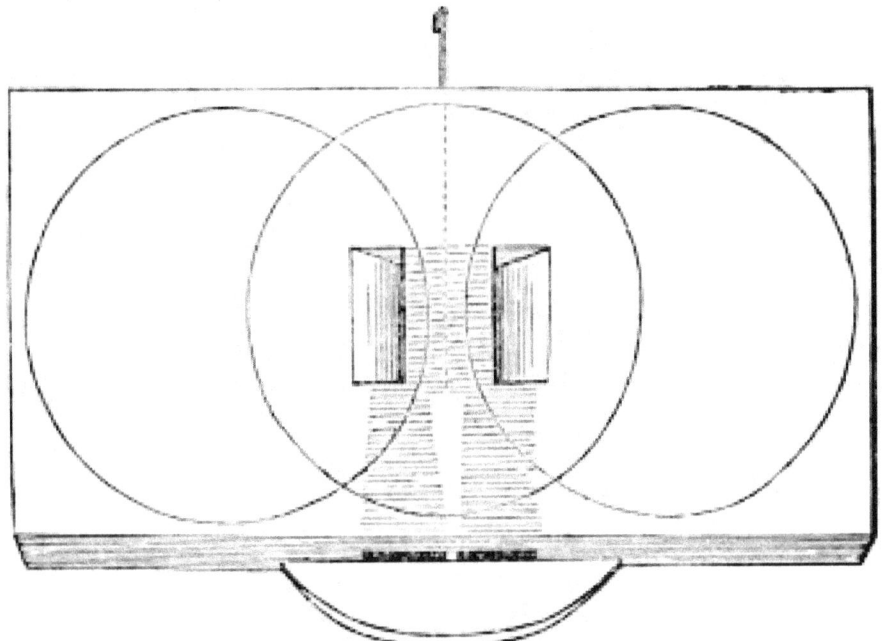

When it is required to take away one of the hives, the communication below must be cut off between them. This is done by means of a divider of strong tin, copper, or iron, pushed in from behind, in a groove cut edgewise in the bottom side of the main board, and resting on the under one. The dotted line in the engraving shows the position of the divider, which must in depth be the same as the passage between the two hives, so as, when in its place, to stop it entirely across the centre.

Another plan of working hives side by side is shown below, two boards being required.

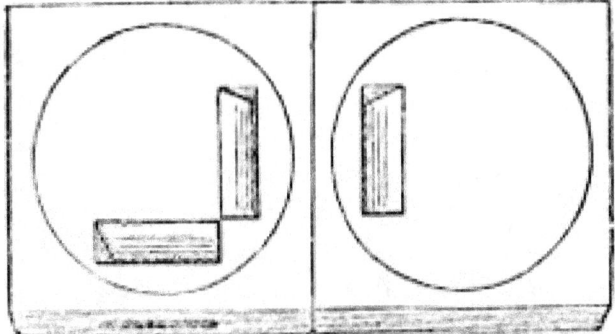

They are made on the double plan, as described at page 45; alike in size and thickness, with the entrance passages cut out from beneath. There must, however, be two entrances to the board intended for the second hive—one in front, and the other at the side, with doorways not less than six inches wide. A wedge or two of wood will contract them as needed. When room is required, the first board with its hive must be moved so far sideways that the second one can precisely occupy its place. At the same time it must be turned half round, so that its mouth and that on the side of the new hive meet and fit close together. The bees will pass into the other hive on going out: on returning it will be the same, for the alighting-board (which ought to be a fixture) will remain as usual. On removing a full hive, the other must be restored to its original position.

WHITE'S COLLATERAL HIVE.

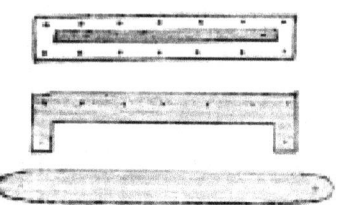

As regards collateral bee-boxes, we owe our original acquaintance with them principally to White, nearly a century ago.[L] His plan requires two boxes, placed side by side, with means of communication, open or stopped at pleasure. These hives do not appear to have been very extensively used; perhaps a good deal owing to the imperfect way in which they were made. For my own use, I endeavoured to improve upon the original design, of which the engraving following will give an idea. The boxes and their boards are shown a little separated; the passages from one to the other being made along the top and bottom of each box. These openings can be closed by the introduction horizontally of slides of thick tin or copper, of an inch and a quarter wide, inserted from behind; let into the boxes their own thickness, and there loosely kept by cases or strips of tin, cut to correspond with the openings. The tins may be about two and a half inches wide. Their form, and that of the slides, is here shown.

[L] See 'Collateral Bee-boxes; or a new, easy, and advantageous method of managing

Bees.' By Stephen White, Holton, Suffolk, London, three editions, 1756, 1763, and 1764.

NUTT'S COLLATERAL HIVE.

The modes we have hitherto noticed as applicable to hives worked side by side suppose two to be employed; but Nutt, a few years ago, introduced *three* boxes, as forming a set; and these hives had their day, where cost and space were not objects.[M]

[M] See 'Humanity to Honey Bees.' By Thomas Nutt.

The three boxes are placed together collaterally, with an entrance from the centre box to the side ones, each way, through what may be termed a grating; which communication can either be open, or cut off by means of a divider, made of sheet tin, pushed between. The centre box Nutt named the *Pavilion*, into which the bees must be hived, and not afterwards disturbed. As more space is required by the bees, it is given by withdrawing the divider. They then take possession of one or both of the side boxes, which when filled can be removed. There are holes on the top of the side boxes for the reception of ventilators. In the construction of these hives the theory of Nutt supposes that a warmer temperature is required in the seat of breeding from that in which comb-building and the storing of honey ought to take place, than which no greater fallacy is possible, as during the formation of a comb the bees cluster round it in masses, to generate the highest degree of warmth. By the agency of ventilation in his side boxes, these are injuriously rendered cooler than the centre one; a thermometer inserted within the ventilator determining the relative degrees of heat.[N]

[N] Another point on which Nutt laid much stress may be mentioned, viz., the supposed advantage to the bees in working on one level, without the necessity of *climbing*, as in storified hives. I long thought this was indisputable. Further consideration led me more minutely to examine the habits of the bee in this respect, and I became convinced that nature had given it equal facilities for moving in every direction. A scientific correspondent thus writes on this subject: "I once propounded the question to a very eminent mathematician, and his reply was, that, if any, the difference was too minute to admit of calculation between the horizontal and the perpendicular movement; it was, in the language of the present day, infinitesimal." Although few of Nutt's positions have been found to stand the test of practice, it ought not to be said that his crude speculations and rash assertions have been altogether without useful results, as they undoubtedly led to farther investigation, and several modern improvements had thus their origin.

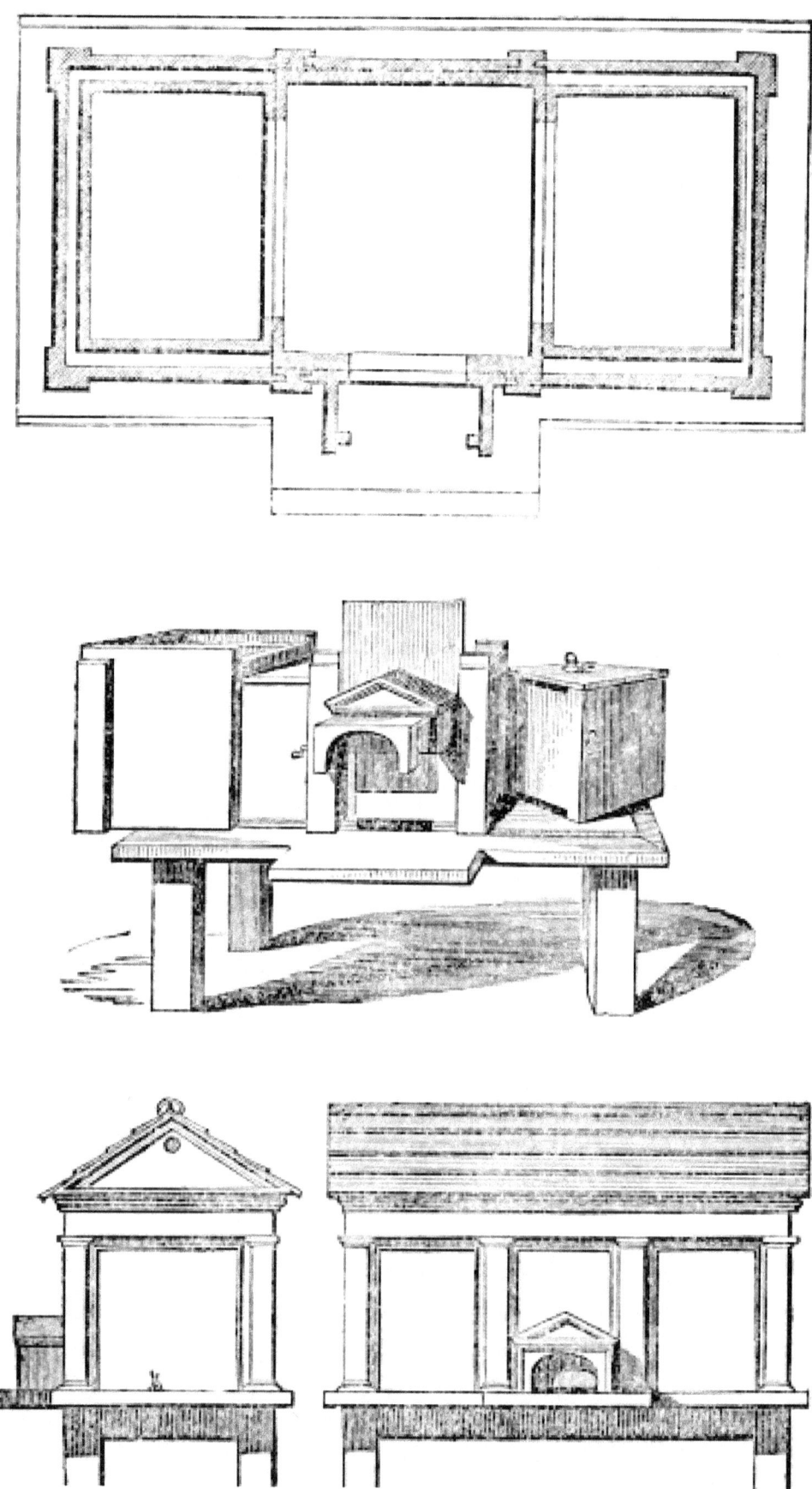

Although at one time I inclined to the principle propounded by Nutt, yet in the working of his hives, I found several disadvantages in their details. I therefore, for my own convenience, altered in part the form, and mode of communication between the boxes, as shown in White's hive; in the absence of a bee-house, completing the fabric by the addition of an outer cover and weather-boarded roof. The details of this hive have so frequently been repeated in former editions, that a reference to the preceding engravings will now suffice to give a general idea of the ground and separated plan, and elevation.

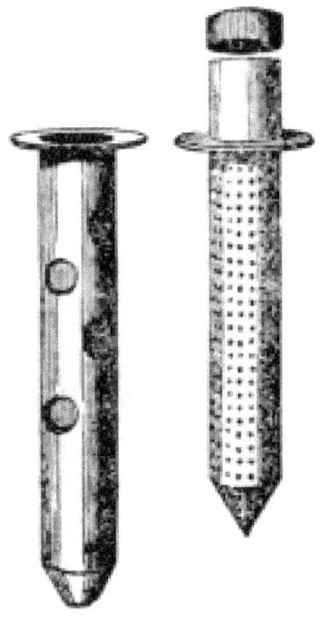

The ventilators I constructed for my Nutt's hive, after trying various forms, consist of double tin or zinc tubes, both resting on a flanch or rim, in the holes prepared for them on the top of the box, usually near the back. The outer tube is of one inch diameter, and six inches long, with six half-inch holes dispersed over it. It is soon fixed down in its place by the bees, and so must remain. The inner tube is of perforated zinc, with a projecting top as a handle, and a cap to put on or off this, as required. The bees will stop up the inner tube where they can get at it, when it may be turned round a little to present a new surface. When wholly stopped, it can be withdrawn from its place, and a clean tube substituted. A small thermometer fits within the inner tube. The scientific apiarian, with experimental objects in view, will often find this kind of apparatus, which is applicable to any plain box-hive, of use.

There is nothing to prevent the adoption, in this hive, of an entrance from beneath the floor-board, in the way described at page 45. In this case, the portico and its adjuncts are superseded; as seen below, in an improved elevation.

NADIR HIVE.

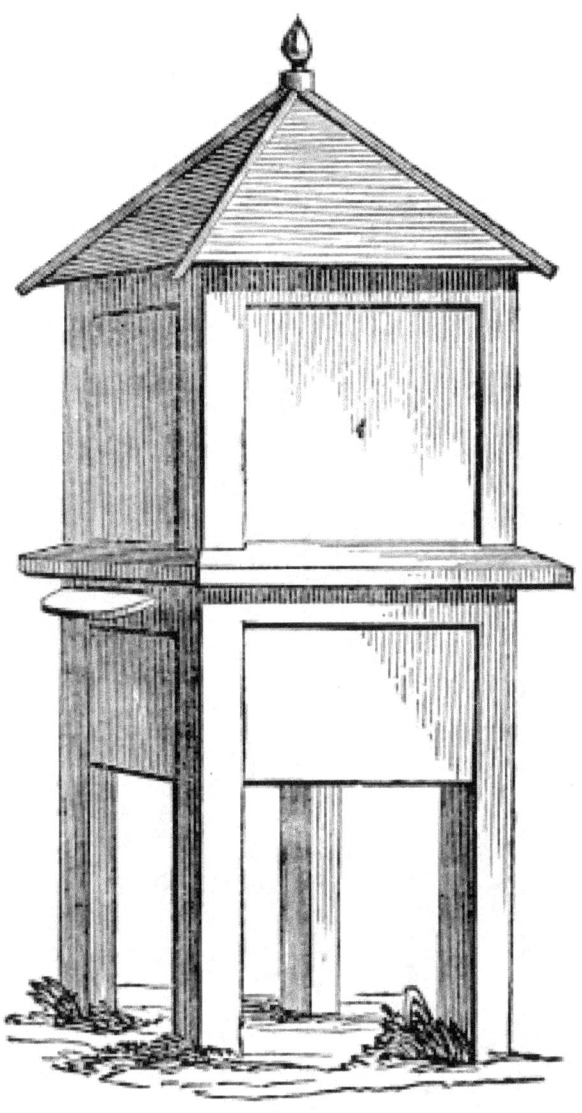

Elevation

Bees not unfrequently take advantage of a hole or crack in the floor of their domicile to commence building combs underneath it, a position possessing some advantages. Deriving a hint from themselves, I contrived what, from this peculiarity, I used to term by way of distinction a *Nadir Hive*, the store box being placed underneath the stock, coming out at the back, as a drawer. The details of construction of the *Nadir Hive* have appeared several times in our former editions, but by way of illustrating the principle and methods of its application, the engravings annexed will not be without their utility. In practice I found no indisposition on the part of the bees to enter and work in the store drawer, into which they have access through the floor-board above, and which is in part made like that shown at page 78. It will be seen that the entire design supposes an out-door hive, with a hipped cover. The stock-box is enclosed by four panels, moving up and down in grooves or rabbets, cut in the corner pilasters, the latter being attached to the box.

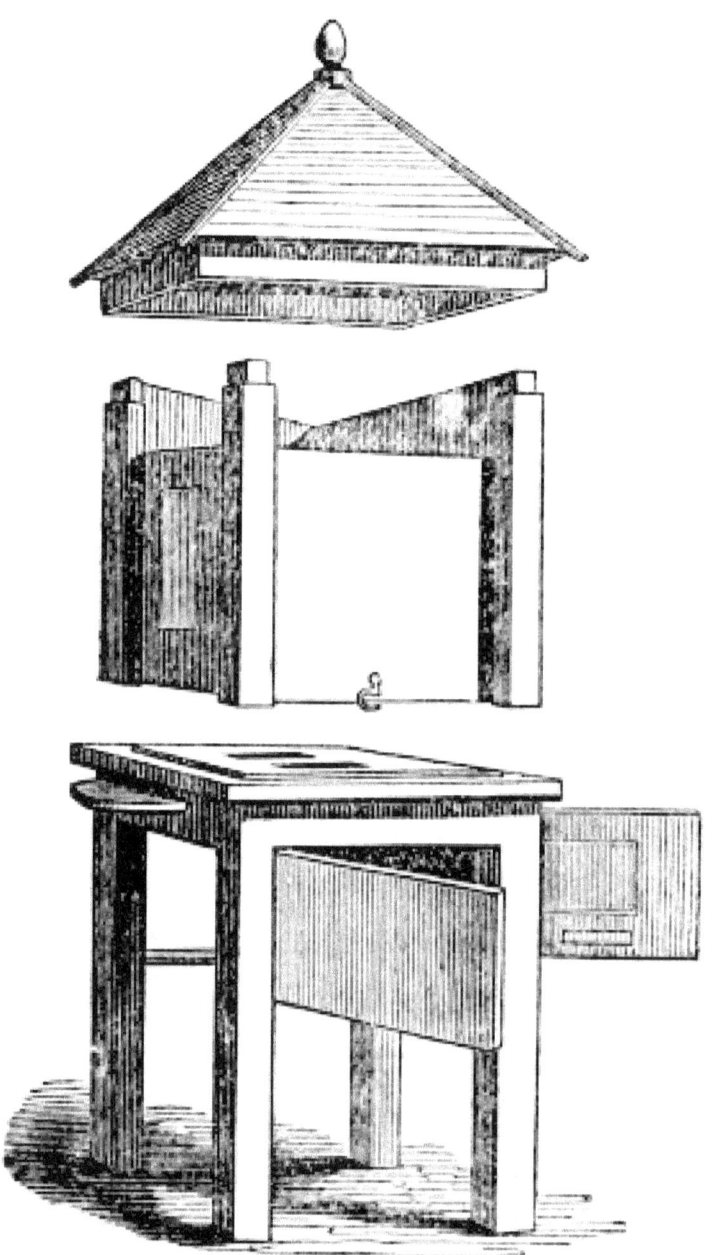

Separated Plan.

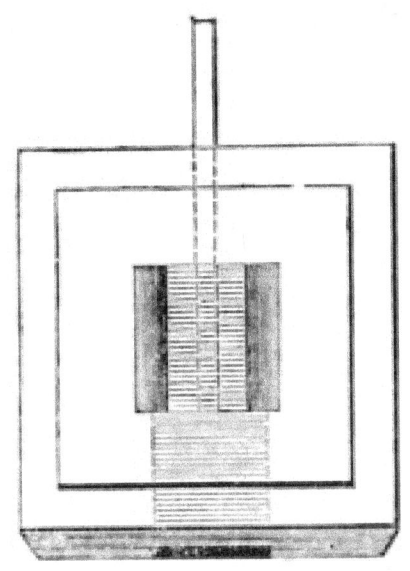

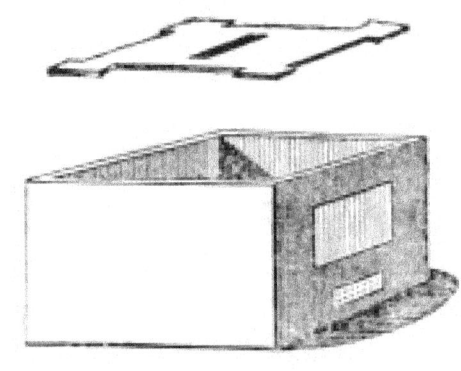

Floor-board.

Nadir drawer and loose cover.

This mode of applying the Nadir, or rather Nether principle, must not be confounded with the usual plan of disturbing the stock-hive for the purpose of placing an empty one beneath it, with a new entrance in the latter for the bees. Under such circumstances the Queen will commonly descend and breed in the nadir, which is converted into the stock, occasioning much subsequent inconvenience. I have not found such to be the case where the stock, and the entrance into it, is not interfered with; and am inclined to believe that this adaptation of bottom-hiving is worthy of much more attention than it has received; to say nothing of its simplicity, safety in management, and obvious convenience to the bees. I will therefore proceed to show in what way it may be made applicable, generally, to the purposes of an apiary.

We have just pointed out that the mode we are now discussing differs from the Nadir principle, and by way of distinction, the term *Nether* will be used, not only to mark the difference, but as presenting a contrast to the opposite word *Super*.

We are to suppose that the shelf on which the hives are ranged in a bee-house is perforated under the centre of each, from back to front, with an opening through, three inches long, and about three quarter inch wide. The hive-board must be a separate loose one; and it ought to lie flat on the shelf, with a perforation similar to the other, the holes in each coming together: to ensure this the shelf can be marked. By moving the hive-board (which is best square) a little sideways of this mark, the position of the two holes is altered, and the communication downwards becomes stopped; always doing this cautiously, to avoid injuring the bees. Or, the same object is perhaps better attained by means of a narrow zinc or tin slide, inserted from behind, between the two boards, moving in a groove ploughed its own thickness out of the shelf. A reference to our last engraving sufficiently exhibits a box, or rather drawer (of suitable size), which, when in its place, moves close on the underneath side of the bee-house shelf, by means of blocks and runners; drawing out at the back by a handle. It may have a window and shutter, but no entrance for the bees, except downwards through the cover, in which is an aperture, corresponding in size and position with those in the boards above it. It will be seen that the cover of the drawer is a moveable one, of half inch board, fitting down flush into it, and resting at the four corners upon wire supports, or small blocks, placed the thickness of the cover, across the angles. The edges of the cover (except at the corners) are cut away just enough to admit of passing a knife-blade down, to separate the combs from the sides, when the whole may be lifted up, with the combs attached. The honey thus obtained is of the purest kind, and I have known a large quantity made available with the least possible disturbance to the bees, on removal. The drawer may be sometimes further made useful for the purpose of feeding, a trough being placed in it, close up to the opening in the cover. A small opening or perforation, at or near the bottom of the drawer, will give ventilation should it be needed.

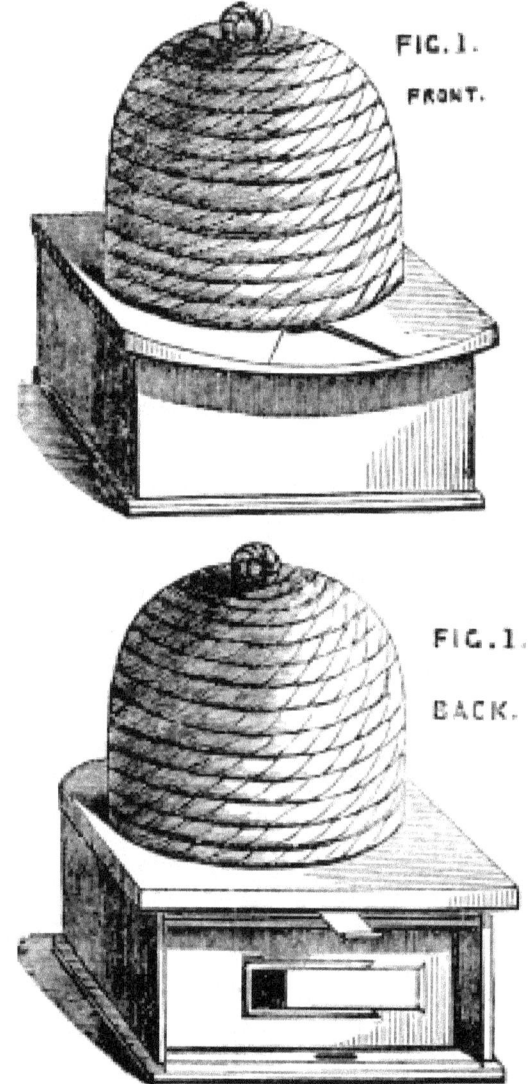

FIC. 1.

FRONT.

FIC. 1.

BACK.

With a further view of facilitating the practice of under-hiving, when favorable circumstances allow of it, we will proceed to describe what I have termed a *Nether*, which may be used as an adjunct to a straw or any other hive, as shown in the illustrations Fig. 1, back and front. It may be of half inch wood, 11 or 11½ inches square withinside, and 6 to 7 inches deep, as circumstances require (see Fig. 4). It has a window and shutter at the back, but neither a fixed top nor bottom, these being moveable boards, of half inch wood, made to project half an inch beyond the Nether box; except that, as respects the bottom board, the projection is increased at the back, with a view to give facilities on the removal of the Nether. (See Figs. 3 and 5.) To receive and enclose the Nether, there is an outer case or cover, also of half inch wood, 13 to 13½ inches square withinside, made half an inch higher than the Nether, its top and bottom boards inclusive.

The outer case is closed on all sides except the top and back. (See Fig. 2.) Upon it rests the floor-board of the stock-hive, which may be of inch wood, showing a projection all round of an inch, except at the front, where an additional three inches is given, to form the alighting board, this part bevelling forwards. A square of half inch wood must be screwed to the underside of the floor-board, of a size to drop easily within the square of the outer case, and thus retaining it in its place. Between the two pieces of which the floor-board is composed, a groove is ploughed out, from front to back, two inches wide, to receive a zinc dividing slide, pushing in from behind. An opening, about three inches long, is cut through the floor-board, towards the front, and also through the cover of the Nether, to correspond, so that a passage for the bees can be opened on withdrawing the divider. (See Figs. 6, front and back.)

FIG. 6. BACK

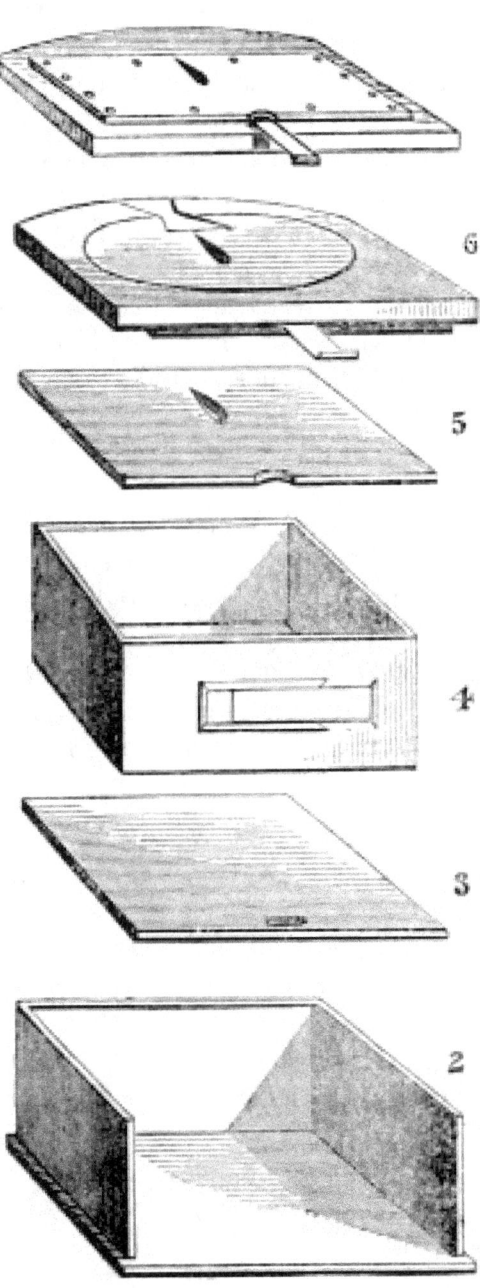

A reversal of this proceeding enables possession or inspection to be had of the Nether box, by withdrawing it (upon its bottom board) from behind, the stock-hive being entirely undisturbed by the operation.

It is well here to remark that experience has shown that it is seldom expedient to apply the Nether principle to any but strong and populous stocks, and especially in only moderately warm weather, as otherwise the bees will prefer to follow the warmth upwards, into a super. On their first admission into the Nether, a few bees will often be lost in consequence of their inability to find the way out, so that, as a precaution, a frequent inspection of the window is at such time desirable. A small aperture behind, at the bottom or side of the Nether, may be made, as a mode of exit for the prisoners, to be closed at pleasure.

BEE SHEDS AND HOUSES.

Under the head of *Hive-covers* we have shown in what way exposed hives can be protected from the effects of weather; and where only one or two of them are kept, any of these might suffice. The case, however, is altered when a well-stocked apiary is aimed at, requiring a more complete provision for permanent safety. For this purpose, some proprietors like a covered shed or verandah, in a well-screened spot, partially open in the front only. There should be ample space inside for a passage behind the hives, which may be ranged far enough from the front to be beyond the reach of wet and too much sun. At page 49, is given a description of a *Hive-range* well adapted for a position like this.

The common wooden bee-houses, as usually constructed, open in front, and closed altogether behind, retaining the sun's heat as an oven, are objectionable. These are frequently the receptacles of dirt and vermin, and most inconvenient to operate in. It would be an improvement to make them deeper backwards; or with a falling front, moving on hinges, so that the hives can be recessed behind it, away from the influence of weather. At the back should be folding doors, opening from top to bottom, allowing a good access to the hives. For greater convenience, it is best only to have them in a single row, with good head room. But a still more desirable plan is to board up the front of the house entirely, making oblong openings through for a passage to the bees, with an exterior alighting board, a good deal slanted downwards (the bees preferring this to a flat surface). The hives are arranged immediately behind, upon a shelf, the further apart the better, as the bees occasionally mistake their own homes, and fall a sacrifice in consequence. This kind of house is capable of receiving some architectural form; and, with locked doors at the back, gives better security than most others against depredation; for hive-stealing is by no means rare, in many localities.

A spare room in a dwelling or an outhouse may often be fitted up to serve the purpose of an apiary, with great convenience; but a lower room is to be preferred, as bees placed at a high elevation often fly a long distance before they alight when swarming, or, perhaps, may settle on the top of a tree. A shelf can be fixed along the wall, with perforated passages facing the hives, leading outside. Any space there may be between the mouth of the hive and the wall should be filled up by means of a suitably formed wooden block or covered passage, well hollowed out on the underneath side; admitting the bees freely through it into their dwelling, but excluding them from the room itself, and thus ensuring safety in operating. Even at a common window, I have sometimes placed a stock-hive on a doubling-board; the latter fitting within the frame of the window, which is raised, to admit of its being projected under the lower edge, so that the bees have no admission except to their domicile.

POSITION AND ASPECT.

As regards position, it is of great importance that an apiary should be as free from damp, or the drippings of trees, and as little exposed to the direct influence of the wind as possible, for which end a sheltered nook on a low level is preferable to an elevated one. A dry gravel, or well-mown grass plot, is often to be preferred; closed in with evergreens, especially the laurel and laurustinus, which are much resorted to by the bees; but always leaving an approach at the back of the hives. Let these not be placed too near water, into which the bees are apt to fall or be blown; and it is desirable that they should be within sight of some dwelling-house, to prevent losses in swarming time. The absence from noise and of bad smells ought to be studied; for no sense in bees is so acute as that of scent. Disturbers of any kind, as fowls, dogs, pigs, &c., should be kept at a distance. Experience has shown that where bees are very extensively kept, the apiary is best divided on the same premises, so as not to have the whole crowded together; often inconvenient, particularly in the season of swarming. Nothing high enough to obstruct the direct flight of the bees should be allowed immediately in front of the hives; but a few low plants are rather useful as resting-places; for bees, from fatigue, often fall to the ground just on reaching home, especially in an evening, and numbers in consequence fall a prey to cold, and various enemies. Many lives may be saved by spreading out a cloth or mat in front of a hive, when this is observed. Shrubs or bushes, at no great distance, are convenient in the swarming season for the bees to alight upon; and often prevent a longer flight, or collecting on high trees, &c.

As regards aspect for bees, many and conflicting have been the recommendations relative to it, influenced by locality and climate. So many circumstances have to be taken into account, that it is difficult to lay down any rule of universal application, and they have been known to prosper in all positions, from due south to north. We know that it has been sometimes advised to turn the hives from the sun in winter, and to screen them from its direct rays in summer: this has led to an opinion that a permanent north aspect is the best; and often it is so. Still local considerations must have their weight, and we are to look to these as regards shelter from cutting winds; the more necessary where no sun reaches the front of the hives. A north aspect need not necessarily be an exposed one in winter; nor at other times one wholly uninfluenced by the effects of the sun. We have recommended doors at the back of a bee-house, by opening which at proper times, in the case of a north frontage, the sun's rays have access from behind, with sufficiently good effect in producing a genial general warmth. In forming a decision as to aspect, we ought to take into account the position of buildings, trees, &c., for we have already observed that the flight of the bees from the hives should be uninterrupted. Moreover, the kind of house must have its weight in the scale; for where this is one closed at the front from the immediate influence of the sun, aspect is of less importance. Dr. Bevan placed his hives around the interior of an octagon erection, without perceiving any sensible difference in their well-doing. It may, however, be remarked that, occasionally, in a hive exposed to the earliest rays of the sun, the bees have been prematurely tempted out in the spring months, and fallen victims to the effects of a damp and chilly atmosphere.

When once fixed, do not move your bees, the mischief of which is self-evident. I cannot enforce this recommendation better than Gelieu has done. "I have seen people," says he, "shift about their hives very inconsiderately; but change of place invariably weakens them, as the bees will return to their old residence, the environs of which are so familiar to them. A hive should remain as fixed to the spot as the ancient oaks, in the hollows of which they delight to establish themselves; where they have their young, their companions, their beloved queen, and all their treasures. When the young bees take wing for the first time, they do it with great precaution, turning round and round, and fluttering about the entrance, to examine the hive well before taking flight. They do the same in returning, so that they may be easily distinguished, conducting themselves nearly after the same manner as the workers of a newly-hived swarm. When they have made a few excursions, they set off without examining the locality; and returning in full flight will know their own hive in the midst of a hundred others. But if you change its place you perplex them, much the same as you would be if, during a short absence, some one lifted your house and placed it a mile off. The poor bees return loaded, and, seeking in vain for their habitation, either fall down and perish with fatigue, or throw themselves into the neighbouring hives, where they are speedily put to death. When hives are transported to a considerable distance, there is no fear that the bees will return. But this inconvenience would be sure to take place if they were removed only a few hundred paces from the spot they have been accustomed to. The hive may not perish, but it will be greatly weakened. In my opinion, if the situation is to be changed at all, they should be taken at least a mile and a half." This removal should only be attempted in winter or early spring, under usual circumstances. It might, however, happen that it was required to move a hive only a very short distance, in the summer time; when no harm would arise were the change of location made by daily shifting it a few inches.

BEE PASTURAGE, AND NUMBER OF HIVES.

It is almost needless to say that on the nature and extent of the vegetable productions, following in succession, in the immediate neighbourhood of an apiary, must mainly depend its prosperity. After every care has been bestowed on all points of housing and management, it is in vain to expect a large harvest of honey where nature has limited the sources of supply, or restricted them to a particular season of the year. The most highly-cultivated corn districts are rarely so favorable to bees as those in which wild commons, woods, and heathy moors prevail; or where some such farm products as Dutch clover, trefoil, saintfoin, buck-wheat, tares, mustard, colewort, turnip and cabbage blossoms, &c., do not enter largely into the staple of the country. The neighbourhood of certain kinds of willows, and of hazels, in the opening spring, is of great advantage to our little collectors in furnishing farina; as also the blossoms of the furze, broom, bramble, wild thyme, &c. To these we may add the large early stores of honey and farina available from many of the products of our horticultural gardens and orchards, as gooseberries, currants, raspberries, apples, pears, plums, and other fruits. Payne says, "I have always found the advantage of planting in the vicinity of my hives a large quantity of the common kinds of crocus, single blue hepatica, helleborus niger, and tussilago petasites, all of which flower early, and are rich in honey and farina. Salvia memorosa (of Sir James Smith), which flowers very early in June, and lasts all the summer, is in an extraordinary manner sought after by the bees; and, when room is not an object, twenty or thirty square yards of it may be grown with advantage. Origanum humile, and origanum rubescens (of Haworth), and mignonette may also be grown. Cuscuta sinensis is a great favorite with them; and the pretty little plant anacampseros populifolium, when in flower, is literally covered by them. Garden cultivation, beyond this, exclusively for bees, I believe answers very little purpose."

It will follow as a matter of course from what we have said, that the size of an apiary in any district must be mainly determined by circumstances. In some seasons, so prolific a harvest of blossoms and honey comes all at once, that a large number of hives may abundantly be filled together. The locality must be the chief guide; and I have known instances where fewer stocks would have yielded a much better return; for one rich colony is worth more than two or three half-starved ones.

The distance to which bees will resort during the honey harvest has been the subject of controversy; some limiting their flight to one mile, and others extending it to three or four. When pressed for stores, they will doubtless fly a long distance, directed probably by their very acute sense of smell; but I am inclined to believe, with Dr. Dunbar, that the ordinary range of their excursions is comprised within the radius of a comparatively small circle.

SUMMER MANAGEMENT.

The question has often been put to me, "How and at what time can an apiary be best commenced?" Some remarks in reference to this subject will be found under the heads both of *Autumnal* and *Spring Management*. At present the reader is supposed to have been put in possession of a prime swarm, in the season, which is the best method of stocking a new hive of whatever kind, and the earlier the better.[O] On this head we may with advantage quote the words of Mr. Golding. "Notwithstanding," says he, "all that has been said about tenanting hives by the removal of the bees of other hives into them, there is no plan so safe or certain as peopling them by good early swarms. When these are brought from a distance, it should be on the day in which they are hived, and in a cloth of coarse texture, which should be tied round near the bottom of the hive, so as to prevent the escape of the bees. Tie up the cloth by its corners over the top of the hive; and, if carried by the hand, or properly suspended, a swarm may be removed in this manner for miles."

[O] All careful bee proprietors will take the precaution to record the weight of the empty hive, and of its floor-board, before stocking it; a matter of subsequent importance in ascertaining the contents. A journal, also, recording dates, and the various operations of the hive, as they arise, will be useful in many ways.

All experienced apiculturists know that no colony of bees thrives, or works so well, as one that is populous at the outset. Should any doubt exist on this point, it is often expedient to unite a second smaller swarm to the first, but this can only be attempted within a few days, before many combs are made, or mischief would result. Our recommendation applies with greater force in a late season, or to the case of second swarms, which are rarely strong enough, separately, to collect sufficient winter stores. Of the mode of proceeding in effecting these junctions we shall hereafter speak, when treating of Uniting Swarms, under the section *Spring Management*.

The plan originally proposed in the Bee-keeper's Manual supposes, as has before been intimated, an arrangement embracing directions for the management of an apiary, "according to the order of the seasons." Our legitimate commencement, therefore, must practically date from the separate existence of the recently established colony; noticing, as we proceed, the various substances stored or used in a hive, and collected more or less abundantly, according to circumstances and season.

Should the weather now be fine, operations are commenced with astonishing activity, the bees being at first solely intent on preparing their new dwelling for its intended objects—the rearing of young, and storing supplies for the future requirements of the family. If, however, circumstances are such as to prevent them from quitting the hive for several successive days following swarming, and before provision is accumulated, recourse to feeding becomes expedient, or starvation might ensue. Under any circumstances, some apiculturists have advised giving honey, or a syrup of sugar, to a newly-hived colony. It is well known that, on leaving the parent stock, the bees carry with them a good deal of honey. There is little doubt that the main object in this provident proceeding is to enable them at once to commence the work of building: this they do almost as soon as they are hived, a piece of comb being frequently made on the same day, which is as quickly appropriated, either as a receptacle of honey or of eggs, if the Queen is already fertile. Where a young Queen has accompanied the swarm, such is not always the case, and this occasions a delay in laying of several days.

The entrance of the hive should now (and at all times when the bees are at full work) be opened to its whole extent.[P]

[P] To the spectator the view of a recent swarm is animated in the extreme, and probably suggested the

SONG OF THE BEES.

We watch for the light of the morn to break, And colour the gray eastern sky With its blended hues of saffron and lake; Then say to each other, "Awake, awake! For our winter's honey is all to make, And our bread for a long supply." Then off we hie to the hill and the dell, To the field, the wild-wood and bower; In the columbine's horn we love to dwell, To dip in the lily, with snow-white bell, To search the balm in its odorous cell, The thyme and the rosemary flower. We seek for the bloom of the eglantine, The lime, pointed thistle, and brier; And follow the course of the wandering vine, Whether it trail on the earth supine, Or round the aspiring tree-top twine, And reach for a stage still higher. As each for the good of the whole is bent, And stores up its treasure for all, We hope for an evening with hearts content, For the winter of life, without lament That summer is gone, with its hours misspent, And the harvest is past recall!

Wax and Combs.—The material of which the combs are so curiously formed is wax, *secreted by the bees* themselves, and not any substance directly conveyed into the hive, as is generally, but erroneously, supposed. Its component parts are carbon, oxygen, and hydrogen. To enable them to form this secretion, the workers must have access to honey or some other saccharine matter; and this is the first thing sought by a new colony. The quantity required is very great, it being estimated that thirteen to twenty pounds are necessary to make one pound of wax. The common opinion is, that the substance often seen adhering so abundantly to the legs of bees is wax, and as such is the basis of the combs. Has it never appeared strange to the observer of a new swarm, that at the time when comb-building is proceeding more rapidly than at any other period, the bees are loaded with but little of this substance? On the other hand, is it not equally clear, that in the early spring, when few or no combs are constructed, they carry it into the hive with the utmost avidity? "To see the wax-pockets in the hive-bee," observes Kirby and Spence, "you must press the abdomen, so as to cause its distension; you will then find on each of the four intermediate ventral segments, separated by the carina or elevated central part, two trapeziform whitish pockets, of a soft membranaceous texture; on these the laminæ of wax are formed, in different states, more or less perceptible." "Whenever combs are wanted," says Dr. Bevan, "bees fill their crops with honey, and, retaining it in them, hang together in a cluster from the top of the hive, and remain apparently in a state of profound inactivity about twenty-four hours. During this time, the wax is secreted, and may be seen in laminæ, under the abdominal scales, whence it is removed by the hind legs of the bee, and transferred to the fore legs; from them it is taken by the jaws, and after being masticated, the fabrication of comb commences." An extraordinary degree of heat always accompanies comb-building, supplied no doubt by the large quantity of oxygen at that time generated.

"In the height of the honey season," Dr. Dunbar observes, "in one day the bees will construct no fewer than 4000 cells. The whole structure is so delicately thin, that three or four of their sides, placed upon one another, have no more thickness than a leaf of common paper." The best authorities have estimated that about half a pound of wax is yielded to fifteen pounds of honey.

The form and number of the combs in a hive vary considerably, the bees adapting them according to the shape of their domicile, so as to fit and fill in every part, and often very irregularly. At first they are beautifully white, but soon, from the heat of the hive, become tinged, and finally turn nearly black. The worker-breeding cells are made the first: they are invariably hexagonal in form, and of one uniform size and depth; but those intended only for the storing of honey are often somewhat larger and elongated; sometimes more so on one side than the other. A small dip or inclination upwards is given to the cells, the better to prevent the honey from running out, assisted, moreover, by a small bar or thickened border of wax, at the entrances. The cells in which the drones are bred are larger in diameter than the common ones, and they are generally placed nearer the outside of the hive, though occasionally joined on to the others. When this takes place, our little architects have the sagacity to interpose two or three rows of cells of an intermediate size, gradually enlarged to the proper dimensions. In this, as in everything else, the bees adapt their operations according to circumstances; constructing their combs, either by suspending them from the top of their dwelling, or occasionally by working them from the bottom, upwards

.

Propolis.—To attach the combs firmly in their place, the bees employ a pliable substance of balsamic odour, called *propolis*, a glutinous exudation from certain trees, or their buds, of a grayish colour, which they collect immediately on swarming, blending with it a portion of wax. With this material they varnish the lids of the closed honey-cells, glue up all crevices in the hive, and cement it down to the floor.

Honey.—We have seen that the first want of the swarm is honey, for the purpose of comb-building. This valuable article the bees collect, by means of their proboscis, from the nectaries of certain flowers, from whence it derives a higher or less degree of flavour, together with its colouring matter; sometimes nearly transparent, to various shades of brown. They receive it into their first stomach or honey-bag, the greater portion being subsequently regurgitated into the cells, employing for the purpose those of both workers and drones. As these become severally filled, they are coated over or sealed with a thin covering of wax. The honey-cells, when thus closed, are distinguishable from those containing brood, by being whiter in appearance, and often slightly concave. The brood-cells are more coloured, besides being a little convex. In some seasons honey is abundantly collected when in the state of what is termed *honey-dew*, a viscous substance found adhering to the leaves of particular trees, especially the oak. This only occurs in certain years, for in others it is found very sparingly, or not at all.

Pollen, or Farina.—The hive will be rapidly filled with combs, and progressively with an increased population, for the eggs, as we have seen in page 13, are matured in three weeks. In the mean time, the bees will have commenced a new labour—that of collecting pollen or farina. This is the anther-dust of the stamina of flowers, varying in colour according to the source from whence it is derived; and it may be remarked that the bees in their collection never mix together the pollen of different plants, but in each excursion visit only one species of flower. By a peculiar adaptation, they are enabled to brush this off, and pack it into the spoon-like cavities (or baskets as they have been termed), furnished for this object, on the centre joint of their hind legs; being often, as has been already pointed out, mistaken for wax. The powder or meal thus conveyed into the hive is by other bees afterwards kneaded up into paste, and stored for use in the worker cells, adjoining those containing brood. To preserve it from the air, a small portion of honey is put on the top of each cell, coated over with wax. Thus prepared, it is a very heavy substance; and this often leads to a false estimate of the value of a hive; for the annual collection of pollen has been variously estimated at thirty to one hundred pounds in a single family.

Naturalists are, I believe, pretty well agreed that the store of pollen or farina is used (with a mixture of honey and water) chiefly for feeding the larvæ; though a portion of such compound may form, occasionally, the sustenance of the bees themselves. Indeed, it has been asserted that pollen is often found in the stomach of bees engaged in the fabrication of wax.

Water.—At certain dry periods, but always in the breeding time, bees require a supply of water, which is necessary in preparing the farina and honey for the brood, as well as to enable them to secrete wax. If no pond or brook is within a reasonable distance, a shallow vessel will do, filled frequently to the brim, having a piece of thin perforated wood floating on it and covering the whole surface; or it may be filled with moss or pebbles, pouring in water to the top, and placing it near the apiary. Precaution is necessary, for the bees easily slip into the water and are drowned. So essential is water, that it has been recommended to place a supply, early in the year, within the hive.

Shade.—It has already been observed that out-door hives ought not to be left exposed to the mid-day and afternoon sun in sultry weather; the heat not only rendering the bees extremely irascible, but subjecting the combs to melting, and especially in wooden boxes, with most disastrous consequences. In all such cases it is well, therefore, to give the comfort of a mat, or something of the kind, thrown over them. In the words of Gelieu, "they delight best in thick forests, because they there find a uniform temperature and a propitious shade. It is a mistake to suppose that bees exposed to the sun produce the earliest and strongest swarms: I have often experienced the reverse. Bees like the shade when working, and the sun only when in the fields."

Moths, Wasps, Hornets, and other Enemies.—In the warm summer evenings, bees are often much annoyed by the attempted inroads of moths, particularly the small *Wax Moth (Tinea Mellonella)*, of a whitish gray colour. These are sometimes formidable foes, and their appearance at dusk on the alighting-board is the signal for a commotion. It is difficult to eject them if they obtain a footing in a hive, where they will deposit their eggs, spinning their silken webs, and they now and then increase so as to cause its entire destruction. When these vermin have established themselves, there is no remedy but driving the bees into another hive. To prevent the ingress of these troublesome invaders, it is sometimes desirable for an hour or two in an evening to close the entrance, by placing before it a screen of gauze, wire-grating, or perforated zinc, to be removed at dark.[Q]

[Q] A difficulty sometimes occurs when it is necessary to confine bees, or drive them into the hive, as the alighting-board is often covered with them in an evening, and the numbers are increased on the least alarm. In this case take a small watering-pot, and gently sprinkle the board and entrance, when the bees, mistaking this for rain, will retire withinside.

Poultry, and some kinds of birds, are destroyers of bees; and many, that from weakness or other causes fall to the ground, become a sacrifice to them. In particular, that little marauder, the Blue Tomtit or Titmouse (*Parus major* of Linnæus), must not be tolerated. In summer he will devour bees, and feed his young with them; and in winter he will even try to force an entrance into the hive.[R] Rats and mice must also be guarded against, as well as slugs and snails.

[R] In some parts these birds are very numerous; and poison has been found efficacious, placed at the hive mouth, in little balls of lard, oatmeal, and nux vomica, mixed together.

The nests of wasps ought to be destroyed: from their superiority in strength and activity, they are very annoying, and often destructive, to bees towards the end of summer; and the nuisance must forthwith be met by contracting the entrance to the hive, when the passage is more readily defended.[S] In this place it may be well to draw attention to a very simple mode of dealing with wasps attacking a hive. We shall have occasion hereafter to notice the fondness of bees for barley-sugar: let a piece of this be laid across, or just within, the entrance of the hive, so as greatly to narrow it. This is so attractive to the bees, that they muster at the door in greater force than the wasps durst venture to assail. As fast as the fortification is devoured, it ought to be renewed, and the out-generalled enemy will retire from a hopeless contest.

[S] Amongst well-informed apiculturists an apology might seem to be necessary in referring to so bigoted an author as Huish; but Huber's observations on some of the habits of bees have frequently been the subject of his ignorant ridicule; and particularly where he says that they occasionally erect barricades, for greater security. Mr. Golding has given a confirmation of Huber's assertion. He says, "At the end of summer, a kind of curtain, apparently a compound of wax and propolis, and about a sixteenth of an inch thick, was erected before the entrance of one of my hives; about two inches and a half in length, and half an inch in height, with the exception of a small aperture at each end." Dr. Bevan, in the 'Honey-Bee,' exhibits a drawing of this piece of fortification. My own experience is perfectly conclusive, as the following extract from my journal will show:—"July 31, 1842. Weather fine. Removed a box of honey from a collateral hive. The wasps had been troublesome for some days, and as the entrance to the centre box was left fully open, the bees had contracted it for better defence. A thin wall of what appeared to be propolis was attached from the upper edge of the doorway, extending along its centre, and closing all up but a space of about three quarters of an inch at each end. I never witnessed a more convincing proof of the sagacity of the bees than this beautiful proceeding." So runs my journal; to which I may add, that the entrance to the box, so contracted, was five inches in length, and three eighths of an inch high; or double that of Mr. Golding's. From the hint thus derived from the bees themselves, I constructed the moveable blocks or mouth-pieces described and shown at page 44.

Insects of all kinds, as earwigs, spiders, wood-lice, &c., should be cleared away from the hives and stands, and ants' nests destroyed. Cobwebs must not be permitted to remain, or numerous deaths would ensue to the bees from entanglement in them. In short, we may sum up by a general recommendation of cleanliness, in every way, and the removal of whatever serves as a harbour to dirt and vermin.

Super-hiving.—Should the weather continue favorable for honey-gathering, the colony must be inspected in about three weeks from the time of hiving. Indeed in sultry weather, and where the swarm is a large one, it is often politic to place a glass or small super upon it very soon, as a ventilator, to moderate the temperature, and prevent the clustering of the bees at the mouth of the hive. If the combs are worked pretty nearly down to the floor, and the cells in a good measure filled, no time should be lost in supplying additional working-room; more especially if symptoms of crowding are apparent, for by this time young bees are coming forth. We may here observe that many experienced bee-keepers object to supering in the case of a new colony, preferring to give the requisite room at the bottom, by means of a *Nadir*; which, as the bees carry their stores upwards, often ensures abundance in the stock-hive, the nadir being removed in the autumn. Under the head *Depriving System*, are some remarks as to the mode of using nadirs; as also under that of *Nadir Hive*, and *Nadiring Stocks*.

Bell-glasses.—As these are commonly formed, nothing can be more objectionable: inconveniently high and narrow, a few misshapen combs are all that can be packed into the space; and these are afterwards only to be extracted by a general mash. The same remark applies to all supers, of any material, where breadth of surface enough is not afforded for a large number of bees to cluster and labour at one time. Can it be a matter of wonder, that a chimney-formed vessel should be twice as long in being filled (supposing that the bees do not forsake it) as a broad one, in which a genial warmth is concentrated, and where several combs can be in progress simultaneously? A reversal of the usual proportions, both in straw and glass supers, is therefore to be recommended. The latter may advantageously be from nine to eleven inches across; the depth being about half the diameter: straight at the sides, and flat on the top. A piece or two of guide-comb, slightly melted, and fixed by its edge to the top of the glass, previously made warm, will serve as an attraction; or in a large glass, four or eight pieces, radiating from the centre uniformly, will direct the bees in working with a regular design, producing a pleasing effect. A useful adjunct to a glass is a small circular tube of perforated zinc, having a rim round its upper end, by which it is held suspended within a small hole on the top. It should be long enough to reach nearly down to the level of the floor. To the tube, when a little warmed, a narrow piece of guide-comb will adhere, and act as an attraction to the bees: it will be further useful as a central support to the loaded combs.

Whatever may be said as to the pleasing appearance of glass supers, it is doubtful whether in point of utility and economy they can compete with those of straw, made as directed under the head of "Straw Depriving Hives," and which can readily be packed and sent to a distance, if needed: or shallow supers, as wide as the stock-hive admits, may be cheaply made by means of a wood hoop, three or four inches deep, on which is fixed a thin top, by two or three small screws. These are readily withdrawn, when the top can be lifted up with the combs suspended. Under the head *Circular Wooden Hives* are some remarks on the subject of wood supers.

In the use of Glasses it is always well at first to prevent the escape of warmth, especially at night, till the bees are well established in their new work-room; and the admission of light is best avoided. A little ventilation afterwards, in sultry weather, is desirable; which may be given by slightly wedging up the lower edge of the super. If a double adapter is in use, it is easy to insert a slip or two of tin or zinc between the two boards, so as to keep them a little separated, for the passage of air, when it seems necessary. Sometimes it is even advisable to introduce between the stock and the super a very shallow box, as a moderator of the temperature. I have found, by experiment with the thermometer, that at a temperature between 95 and 100, the combs will soften so much as to be in danger of collapsing.

Triplets and Nadirs.—In good seasons and localities, the first super is sometimes filled in time to admit of the introduction of another (or triplet), on an adapter, observing the rules laid down at page 32. But even where the first super is completely filled, it is often politic not to remove it for a few days, as its attraction induces the bees to occupy the triplet. On the other hand, if from any cause a super has been left only partially filled upon one hive, it may be removed (the bees being first ejected), and placed upon some other for completion. Instead of a separate triplet, an addition may often be made to the first super, especially if of straw, by placing beneath it an eke, consisting merely of two or three bands of the same material; in fact a hoop. This will save the bees the labour of laying the foundations of fresh combs, as they have but to continue the old ones downwards. We may here call attention to what has been said at page 43, respecting the use of box, No. 3, of the bar-hive, and of Nadiring.

After the main honey season is over, which is usually as soon as the dry July weather sets in, it is useless, in most localities, to give any further extension of working room; and, indeed, from the end of this month there is, under common circumstances, often rather a diminution than an increase of store.

In proportion to the wealth of the colony is the determination of the bees to defend it; and their irascibility and vigilance are now greater than heretofore, the strongest stocks showing it the most. The work of the year being pretty well over, all their attention is turned towards home. They become more and more suspicious, and the less they are approached or annoyed the better; for they are slow to forget or forgive an injury.

AUTUMNAL MANAGEMENT.

Much of what has been said in the preceding section is equally applicable in practice to the later periods of the summer. The month of August is usually associated with the collection of harvest. Though this may often hold good as regards honey, yet the storified or doubled stocks of the spring are commonly ready for deprivation at an earlier period, occasionally in May, and so on throughout July; the spring-gathered honey being usually to be preferred in point of quality. I know of no better rule as to the fitness of a super, or side hive, for removal, than an observation of the state of the combs and cells, which ought to be completely filled and sealed over, to prevent a loss of honey by running out. In this stage the sooner it is appropriated the better, as a longer continuance only leads to discoloration. As respects a colony of the same year, Dr. Bevan remarks, "as a general rule, no honey should be taken from a colony the first season of its being planted, though there may be an extraordinary season now and then, which may justify a departure from this rule:" the produce in such a case is usually denominated *virgin honey*, though that term is often applied indiscriminately to any in combs free from brood. But in any event the stock-hive should be previously examined, for there is a disposition in bees to carry their stores into a super, though afterwards they sometimes remove it into the stock-hive. In cases where doubt exists as to a sufficiency of winter store, it is often well to allow them to do this; recollecting the further advice of Dr. Bevan, that, "it should be an invariable rule never to remove an upper box or hive till an under one be quite full; nor to diminish the weight of a stock-box below seventeen or eighteen pounds, exclusive of the box itself."

To remove a full Box or Super.—The middle of a sunny day may be recommended as the best time to take away for deprivation a box or glass of honey. The mode usually adopted is at once to remove it from its position to a distance from the stock-hive, and there get rid of the bees. I have often found it well to reverse this proceeding. Whether the box to be taken is a collateral or storified one, let the communication from the parent hive be previously cut off, and without any jarring. Entire quietness is the main requisite. Gently lift up the super on one side, inserting under it a small wedge or two, so as just to allow an exit for the bees. The position of the queen bee will soon become apparent. If she is not in the super (and she seldom is there after it is filled), the silence that at first prevailed will be exchanged for a murmuring hum, attended by a commotion among the bees; and they shortly after begin to quit the super, without attempting any attack. Should the queen be present, however, a very different scene would ensue, and a hubbub would then commence in the stock-hive; though the loss of their queen is sometimes not discovered by the bees for a considerable time. In such a case, the box must be reinstated in its former position, and the communication reopened till some other day. The process might happen to be complicated by the presence of brood, for this the bees leave very reluctantly, and often not at all. In an emergency of this kind, it is best to restore matters to their previous state, and let the super remain till the brood is perfected. A little patience is sometimes necessary: but all attempts at ejection of the bees by tapping, smoking, or driving usually do more harm than good. So long as they continue to leave the super, it may remain where it is, for on these occasions young bees are sometimes numerous; and if the super is removed, though only to a short distance, these are in part lost, not having become sufficiently acquainted with the position of their home; or, if they enter a wrong hive, they pay the penalty with their lives. This freedom from disturbance has the further good effect of preventing in a great degree the intrusion of robber bees, readily distinguishable from the others by their hovering about the box, instead of flying from it. These are strangers from various quarters, immediately attracted by the scent attending the removal of a full box or glass. Should a few of these plunderers once obtain a taste or sample of the honey, they speedily convey the good news to their associates, when large reinforcements from every hive in the neighbourhood will be at once on the alert, and quickly leave nothing behind but empty combs. Let the separated super, therefore, not be left or lost sight of, but if scented out by robbers, be conveyed into some room or out-building to prevent a general battle; and which might extend itself to all the neighbouring hives. The remaining bees may here be brushed out, escaping by the window or door. Mr. Golding has sometimes found the advantage of using for the purpose a darkened room, with the exception of a very small aperture, to which the bees will fly and make their exit. Others like to remove a super at once to a short distance from the stock-hive, leaving it shut up in perfect darkness, for an hour or two. Its edge is then raised up, when the bees will evacuate it. In the case of a bar-hive super, after most of the bees have left it, it can be placed across a couple of rails or sticks, when the top cover may be unscrewed and detached. It is then readily cleared of bees by brushing them downwards between the bars, with a feather or a twig.

The same general directions apply when a full glass is to be removed. If it stands on a double adapter, a piece of tin or zinc can be inserted between them, and the upper part then lifted with the glass. Payne, however, says, "I have found the process much simplified by placing an empty box between the glass and the parent hive, and leaving it a few hours. The bees by that time have quitted the glass, and by this plan robbing is entirely prevented, whilst the bees are less irritated." It might occasionally happen that a piece of comb had been worked upwards, so as to be connected with the underneath hive, and thus causing a difficulty on attempting a separation. There is no better way of meeting such an emergency than by passing a bit of fine wire beneath the lower edge of the super, from side to side, and thus cutting through the obstruction. It may be well to observe that on removal, the box or glass ought to be kept in its original position, to prevent the honey, which at first is thin and fluid, from running out of the cells, and especially in hot weather.

Honey Harvest.—As regards the quantity of honey to be taken from a hive in any one year, there can, in our uncertain climate, be no general rule, though now and then I have known a very large amount obtained by deprivation.

Payne says, as the result of his own experience with depriving hives, "It is usual to obtain from every good stock twenty or perhaps thirty pounds of honey annually." This would be thought too high an estimate, in many districts; as in my own, near London. It must be remembered that honey thus harvested sells at a higher rate than that procured by suffocating the bees, as in the common single hives; for then the brimstone not only imparts a disagreeable flavour, but there is no means of preventing the intermixture with the honey more or less of pollen and brood. After deprivation, the sooner the honey is drained from the comb the better, as it soon thickens, particularly if not kept warm. For the purpose of straining it off, a hair sieve is commonly used, within which the combs are inverted; the waxen seals on both sides being first sliced off. The honey will of course run off the sooner if placed before a fire, but exposure to heat is injurious to fine flavour. We may here resort to the advice of Payne, who says, "the honey should be put into jars, quite filled, and tied down with a bladder; for exposure to the air, even for a few hours, very much deteriorates its flavour. I may observe that honey in the combs keeps remarkably well, if folded in writing paper, sealed up to exclude the air, and kept dry."

Comb-knives.—A difficulty sometimes arises in extracting the combs from common hives or boxes. A large spatula will separate them from the sides, but to detach them from the top, an instrument of a different kind is requisite. The one often preferred is simply a bar of steel about fourteen inches in total length, half an inch wide, and an eighth of an inch thick. At one end it is bent at a right angle with the handle, and at the other at an angle of 80° or 90°. The part thus turned up is in both cases an inch and a half long, rather less than half an inch wide, and made spear-pointed, or lancet-shaped; sharp on both sides, to cut either way. The one end is used when the top of the hive is flat; and the other is adapted to the common dome-formed roof. Another useful instrument is the one employed in detaching the combs from the bar-hives, made as recommended by Mr. Golding, with a double-edge blade, an inch and a half long, and three eighths of an inch wide; turned at right angles from the end of a rod, which may be of quarter-inch square iron. For occasional convenience, the other end may be turned the flat way, sharpened at both edges.

Robbers.—Should an attack upon a hive from strange bees take place, which sometimes occurs at this season (the strong robbing the weak), no time ought to be lost in narrowing the entrance, for if allowed to continue a day or two the ruin of the family might be the consequence. Indeed, it is always well gradually to do this as the working season draws to a close. An assault from robber bees is often a much more formidable evil than one from wasps, although it is said that one of these is a match for three bees. Unless the colony is very weak, they are usually soon expelled. Not so with bees, for if but one or two strangers gain admittance into a hive they will return again and again, always with an accession of force; and for a day or two it is often necessary entirely to close the entrance against them, opening it only at night. In such case the robber bees will sometimes collect in vast numbers at the mouth of the hive, when a shower from a watering-pot will send them away to dry themselves. The thieves are generally distinguishable; and they are often cunning enough to commence their marauding practices early in the morning and late at night. A supply of honey given on the top, or even sprinkled among the combs of contending hives, will often divert the attention of the combatants; or smoke is sometimes effectual, puffed into both hives. If fighting recommences on the succeeding day, the smoking should be repeated, followed by a feed of honey. Others have found it advantageous to remove for some days a plundered hive to a distance; or even to make the belligerent hives change places in the apiary; which, as a friend remarked to me, "gives a new turn to their ideas of meum and tuum." A German proprietor, after removing an attacked stock, put in its place a hive filled with wormwood leaves, so distasteful to the robbers that they forsook the spot, when the stock was brought back again.

Autumnal Feeding.—All labour is now usually suspended for the year, and it remains to see that ample provision is laid up for the coming winter and spring. There ought not to be less than seventeen to twenty pounds of honey in a hive of the same year; but in the case of an old one, eight or ten pounds more must be allowed in estimating the weight; for old combs are much heavier than new ones; besides that they are a good deal filled with stale pollen, and sometimes contain candied honey, of no use to the bees.[T] In a healthy stock there should be no scarcity of food, if the season has been tolerable. The worst, however, must be provided for; and if, from any cause, it should be necessary, recourse must be had to supplying the deficiencies of nature. "A stock of bees," observes Dr. Bevan, "generally consumes from a pound to a pound and a half of honey per month, betwixt the first of October and the first of March. From this time to the end of May, they will consume double that quantity."

[T] In reference to this part of our subject, it may be useful to quote the following estimate, as given by Dr. Dunbar:—"A common straw hive weighs, when empty, from five to six pounds; an ordinary swarm about four pounds; the wax of a full hive of the current year, nearly two pounds; of the preceding year, at least three pounds; and the farina in the cells, not less than one pound; making in all about fifteen pounds. A stock, therefore, to be secure, ought to be double that weight in the gross; that is, should contain not less than fifteen pounds of honey."— *Naturalists' Library*.

The requisite feeding to make up the winter store ought not to be delayed later than the beginning of October, and the weather should be fine. Food must never be placed in the open air, but under a cover; otherwise the smell would attract wasps or, what is worse, strange bees; in the latter case a battle generally following.

Feeding-troughs.—The feeding of bees, though apparently a simple matter, is often a troublesome process, and without due precaution sometimes leads to a good deal of commotion. The common swarming hives present much difficulty, from their construction. Having no opening at the crown, the clumsy and dangerous mode must be resorted to of bottom-feeding, in any way possible; either by tearing up the hive for every supply of food, or by means of an eke, pushed for the purpose beneath it. An improved hive gives facilities for presenting food on the top, obviating these inconveniences; and where it may be supplied in any quantity, without disturbance; at the same time that it is inaccessible to all enemies.

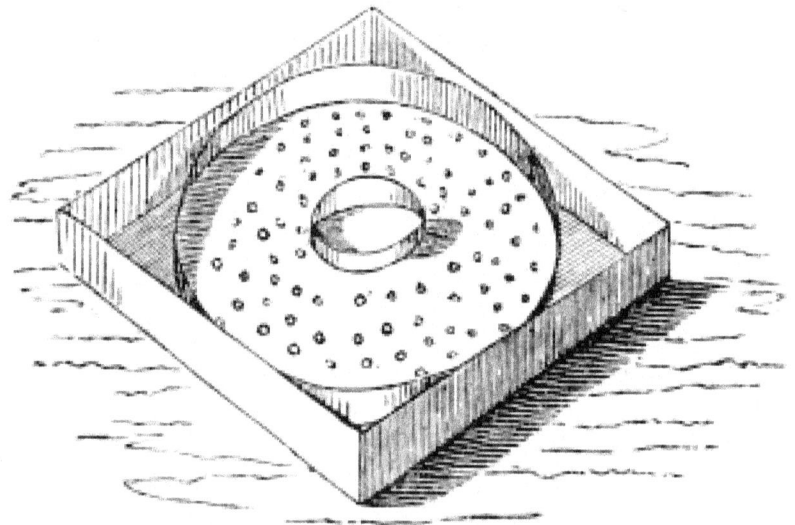

When there is a hole in the centre of the top of the hive, a trough may be used, made of tin or zinc, seven or eight inches square, and one inch and a quarter deep; having a circular two-inch hole in the middle of the bottom, with a rim round it, standing up half an inch, through which the bees enter the pan from below. Another circular rim or partition, as large in diameter as the square of the pan will admit, is soldered down within it at the four points where it touches the sides. It must not go down to the bottom, but a space should there be left of nearly an eighth of an inch, as a passage for the food, which is poured in at the four angles. A perforated thin wooden bottom or float is fitted loosely into the pan, between the circles, removing an objection sometimes made against the chilling effects of metal upon bees. The float should be a little raised by means of two thin strips of wood, appended below, to allow the liquid to flow beneath. A cover is made by a piece of glass, resting on the larger circle, but cut nearly octagonal in form, so as to leave the corners open. The circle on which the glass rests should be an eighth of an inch lower than the outer rim. In making a trough of this kind, it is sometimes customary to append beneath it a central descending rim or tube, fitting down into the hole on the top of the hive. This is worse than useless, and it is in the way on the removal of the pan; on which occasion it is expedient to push beneath it a piece of sheet tin or zinc, to stop the communication from below.

Such a pan is perhaps made more readily without the inner circle; in which case, all that is needed for pouring in the food is a partition going nearly down to the bottom, so as to cut off a portion at one corner. The glass pane can rest on angle-pieces, sunk an eighth of an inch, at three of the corners, and upon the partition at the fourth one, this part being left open.

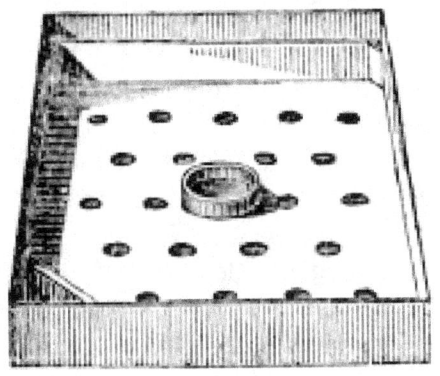

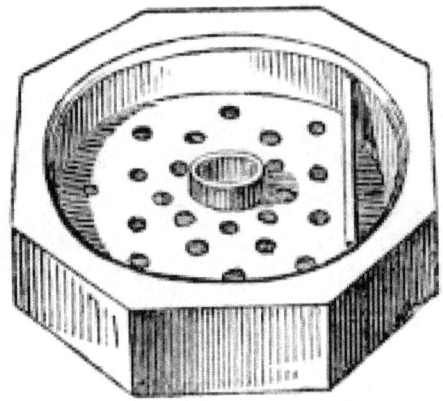

A charge is sometimes brought against zinc feeding-pans, as tending to create acidity in the food. There is perhaps some truth in this, where it is suffered to remain too long; together with another cause of mischief,—a very general neglect of cleanliness. Those, however, who prefer wood altogether may have troughs made of that material, either square or round in form, as that given in our illustration, which is turned from hard wood in a lathe; a piece being divided off on one side by a partition, under which the food passes, beneath a wood float. A pane of glass rests upon a circular rabbet turned out to receive it, leaving uncovered the part beyond the partition.

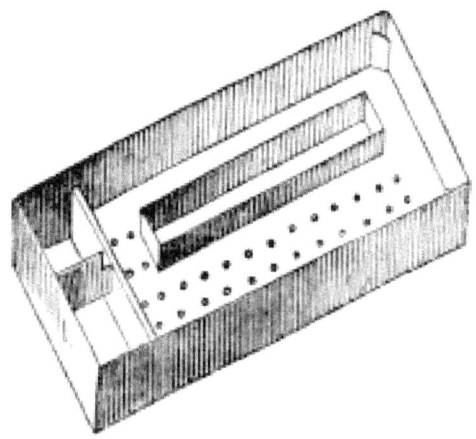

For the purpose of feeding the bees in my bar-hive, a zinc or tin trough is provided, of a form adapted to the position of the openings cut through the crown-board to the stock-box. The extreme length is ten inches and a half, four inches wide, and an inch and a half deep. At one end is a partition an inch and a quarter wide, going down nearly to the bottom. Into this the honey or other food is poured, running under a wooden perforated float, and fitted loosely within the bottom. A pane of glass rests on two angle pieces, at one end, and on the cross division at the other, all sunk a quarter of an inch, and covering the pan as far as the partition. The latter is strengthened in the centre by a cross-stay, against which the glass rests. At the bottom is an opening seven inches long and half an inch wide, with a rim around it, about half an inch high. This opening is placed so as to correspond with that communicating through the bars beneath. Draw out the slides, and the bees will have access to the pan. This proceeding is of course reversed on its removal.

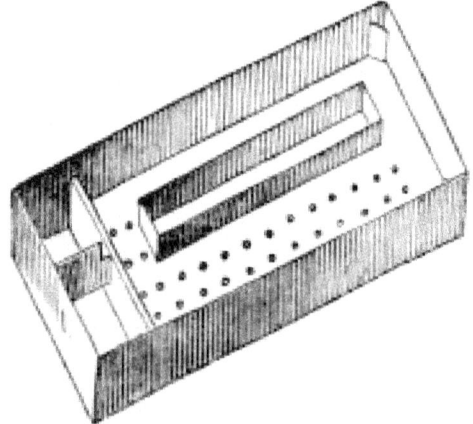

Bee Food.—Nothing that can be presented to bees is so acceptable as their natural food —pure honey. At this season, as it is chiefly stored for future consumption, it is best unmixed with water. Fill the pan every evening till the requisite quantity is given, for it will speedily be emptied. Refuse honey may be given to the bees in the combs, piled in a pan, a little separated, and covered by a box or hive. The sooner the feeding is ended the better, the bees, if in health, being on these occasions much excited and often irascible. Let enough be given when you are about it. Gelieu says, "Let there be no higgling with bees; better that they have too much than too little." Recollect that little of your bounty is now eaten, but is conveyed and stored for the day of need; the bees sometimes extending the combs purposely to receive it, and often of pollen as well; for it is observable that feeding at any time stimulates them to foraging abroad. Nothing is wasted, and whatever there is to spare will be repaid with interest in the spring. It must also be borne in mind, that what food is likely to be wanted must be supplied *now*, for very rarely should any further attempts at feeding be made till the returning spring restores animation to the family. A reference to *Spring Feeding* will supply information as to various substitutes for honey.

Winter Store.—Under the head of *Autumnal Feeding* we have mentioned the usual estimate as to the requisite supply of honey for the winter. Anomalous as it may seem, it has been remarked, that the quantity apparently required is not dependent on the population of the hive. The number of mouths make little sensible difference, even when two or three stocks have been united. This fact was first noticed by Gelieu, and has been corroborated by other observers.

"In doubling the population," says Gelieu, "I naturally conceived that we must also double the quantity of food; for I had always seen that two or three families, living together, used more meat than each would have done singly, however rigid their economy. The more mouths the more meat, thought I; and, in consequence, I augmented greatly the amount of provision the first time that I doubled a hive; but to my astonishment, when I weighed it again in the spring, I found that the united swarm had not consumed more than each would have done singly. I could not believe my eyes, but thought there must be some mistake; nor could I be convinced until I had repeated the experiment a hundred times over, and had always the same result."

This seeming anomaly, Gelieu and others have attempted to account for on the principle that the increased heat of an augmented population is in some measure a substitute for food; but this is opposed to all experience, which proves that warmth is a stimulus to consumption. A more satisfactory way of disposing of the question seems to be, in the first place, that the bees in a well-peopled hive feel in a lower degree the evils consequent on frequent changes of temperature occurring in winter, than is observable in a less populous one; for alternations of cold and warmth have an injurious effect, generally leading to an increased consumption of stores. The next consideration is that the junction of stocks, alluded to by Gelieu, ensures a larger supply of labourers in the early spring. It is not in the cold weather that much consumption of food takes place, but after the month of February, when the great hatching comes on; and then not so much by the *bees*, as by the *brood*. In a thinly-populated hive, almost the whole family is required within-doors at this time, to warm the eggs and feed the young; and consequently little is added to the continually diminishing stock of honey and farina. Nothing is more common than to see a hive, apparently well stored in February, on the point of perishing in the month of April. This is not the case where a large number of bees can be spared to go abroad and bring in fresh supplies, to keep pace with, or even to exceed, the demands of the craving brood.

Autumnal Unions, Fuming, and Transferring Bees.[U]—The subject of autumnal unions of bee stocks is strongly advocated by Gelieu; and in this country has not always received the attention it demands. Perhaps this is in part owing to ignorance as to a ready mode of accomplishing the object; and in some degree from the supposed doubt about maintaining the bees, when collected in a large body, through the winter. The latter difficulty is removed by a reference to what has been said on the subject of winter store, in the last section. I hope I shall be able to show that, by a safe and simple expedient, the bees of two or three weak or worn-out families may be joined together, to form one vigorous stock; at the same time saving thousands of valuable lives. The late Apiarian Society of Oxford is entitled to credit for the care it bestowed on this branch of bee economy; and the method of procedure now to be explained was there successfully practised. It should be done about September, and in warm weather.

[U] It may be well in this place to call attention to the distinction between the system of *Transferring Bees*, in *Autumn*, in the way now pointed out, and what has sometimes been confounded with it; namely, the practice of *Transferring Bees and Combs together*, from one hive to another. This I never advocated, except in bar-hives, when it is sometimes practicable, provided the combs are built in straight lines.

The custom of stupefying bees by some narcotic substance has long been in practice; and, observes Dr. Dunbar, "there is no more useful auxiliary in every operation in an apiary than smoke." By subjecting them to the fumes, the bees are rendered insensible and harmless for a time; but soon recover, with no ill-effects subsequently. Apparatus more or less complicated has been invented for fuming; but perhaps the most simple was that used at Oxford, which is a tin tube, eighteen inches long, and three quarters of an inch in diameter; readily made by any tin-worker. One end is extended and flattened to adapt it to the entrance of the hive, whilst the other is applied to the mouth of the operator. In the centre of the tube is a box, two inches and a half long, and two inches in diameter, to contain the fumigating material; and to receive which, one end is made to draw out like a telescope. The two ends of the box, where the tubes join it, are stopped withinside by divisions of perforated tin. This part must be put together, by rivetting, and without solder, which the heat would melt. An instrument of this form is adapted for most purposes where smoke is needed, it being applicable to fuming a hive at the mouth, or, in some cases, from the top; for it is, occasionally, more in accordance with the object in view that the bees should be driven down, rather than upwards. When, therefore, this is proposed, a bend in the tube becomes expedient, which is readily managed by having the farther end made in two pieces to be disconnected at pleasure, after the plan of a watering-pot. Another end-piece can then be slipped on like a nozzle, turned downwards, to enter the hole through the top of the hive. The instrument just described is of course used in the hand; but another kind is sometimes applicable, made not unlike a pepper-box, upon a foot, which stands on, or in a hole in, the ground, whilst the hive about to be fumed is placed over it. The top lifts off to receive the fungus; and this, as well as the lower end, is pierced with holes.

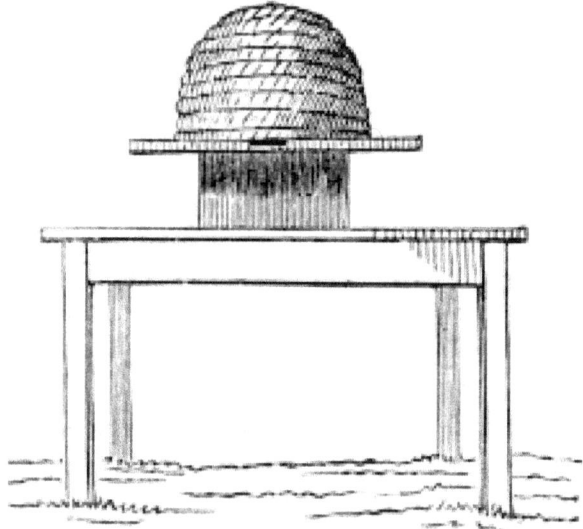

The substance hitherto chiefly recommended for the fumigation or stupefying of bees is a kind of fungus, found growing often very large and round, mostly in rich pastures or plantations, in the autumn. It is the *Lycoperdon Giganteum*, but variously called, as Devil's snuff-box, fuzz-ball, or puff-ball. It should be gathered when nearly ripe. Dry it in the sun, or a cool oven, and preserve it from damp. It is then a spongy substance, containing brown dust; and burns with an offensive smell. The difficulty often of procuring this material led me to make trial of another kind of fungus, called *Racodium Cellare*, or mouse-skin *Byssus*. It may be found growing in large wine or beer vaults, in immense dark-coloured bunches or festoons, suspended from the roof, often wearing a handsome appearance. In a single such vault, in London, I have seen as much as would suffice for a large portion of the bee-keepers in Great Britain; and I can recommend it (not too freely used) as even more efficacious than the other fungus. It requires no preparation, igniting and smouldering readily, and may be preserved for years. Whatever be the material employed, let the box of the tube be about two-thirds full; and a few puffs will cause it to send forth smoke abundantly. The hive which it is intended to deprive of its tenants may be lifted gently from its place soon after dusk, and placed over some kind of receptacle. An empty hive, turned bottom upwards, might answer with a little management, but there must be no place of escape for the bees. The best thing is a box or bowl, about ten inches square withinside, and four or five inches deep; with a wide flat rim all round. The first introduction of the smoke will cause an uproar among the bees, which will speedily be followed by silence, as they fall down from its effect. A minute or two generally suffices for this, assisted by striking the sides and top of the hive. When all is quiet, turn up the hive, and you will have received the greater part of its inhabitants in the bowl, in a stupefied state and perfectly subdued. A portion will remain sticking in the combs, which must be cut out one by one, and the bees swept with a feather into the bowl, where a little more smoke will, if needed, keep them quiet in the interim. As respects the Queen, if perceived, she can be taken away, but the bees will commonly dispose of her in their own way, by the next morning. The whole being thus collected, they soon begin to show signs of returning animation; and when this is about to take place, sprinkle them pretty freely with a mixture of sugared ale. Next, lift quietly from its stand the hive to which the smoked bees are to be united, placing it over the bowl, but leaving no opening except the mouth, for air. The bees from above, attracted by the scent, will go down, and begin licking the sprinkled ones. The whole become intermixed, and ascend together into the hive over them, in perfect goodwill. Leave them till the following morning early, when the bowl will generally be found empty. Replace the doubled hive on its original stand, and the work is complete. If it is thought desirable still further to augment its strength, the bees of a second hive may be added in the bowl; or a second union may be made in a night or two afterwards. All that remains is to see that the hive contains honey to last the winter; and whatever is wanted to make up about eighteen pounds must be supplied for that purpose, in the way pointed out in a previous section.

We will now detail another mode of proceeding, at once speedy and efficacious, and attended with no risk to the operator. With the tube of which we have before spoken, in the evening puff some smoke into the mouth of the hive you wish to take, without removing it. Compel as many of the bees to fall down as you can; then lift the hive, and brush out those remaining; taking away the Queen if you can find her without much trouble. Collect the whole in a heap on the floor-board, and sprinkle them pretty well with sugared ale. You may now, if the numbers are still thought insufficient, add to the first, the smoked bees of a second hive. Next puff some smoke within the stock-hive into which the bees thus collected are to be transferred, quietly where it stands; just sufficient to stupify its inhabitants, and produce a uniformity of scent. Turn it bottom upwards, floor-board and all, so as to drop no bees; and place it, if of straw, in a pail, or some similar kind of support. In this position lift off the floor-board, and sprinkle these bees also with a smaller portion of the ale, in the hive where they are. After this is done, before they have recovered, sweep the smoked bees uniformly among the combs of the hive destined to receive them. Clean and scrape its floor-board, and as soon as symptoms of returning animation begin to appear, replace it, turning the whole again into the right position. All that remains is to restore it at once to its original place or stand. Before the hive is left, clear away from the entrance any bees that may have fallen down, so that the passage for air is not obstructed. In the absence of a tube like the one described, it is very practicable to make use of a common pipe and tobacco; but the latter should be of a mild kind, and not too freely used, or many deaths might ensue.

In selecting the future domicile of the family thus augmented, it will be well to observe that the hive is not one of long standing, in which the combs have become thickened with age. Indeed, a colony of the same year is to be preferred, and more particularly where the Queen is a young one. If, however, it is desired to cut out the old combs from the intended future stock-hive, it can now be done with safety; first turning on to the board as many of the bees as you can. A supply of honey will invigorate the new community, and the vacancies will be filled up with fresh combs, provided the operation has not been delayed too late in the season.

It is of great importance here to observe, that after making autumnal unions, in cases where the bees have been expelled from hives possessing fresh combs, the latter ought to be left undisturbed, as so much gain to a spring swarm, which will gladly accept a house ready furnished: moreover, a vast saving of honey results, for the fabrication of comb, as we have shown at page 110, consumes a great deal of this. The same remark applies to supers partly filled with combs; but they should be kept clean and dry. It is worthy of remark, that some authorities maintain the opinion that bees will now and then re-work portions of old combs or wax, but it must be free from impurity.

As far as it can be managed, it is desirable that attention should be paid to the previous position of the hives intended to form unions, for there is always a disposition in bees to return to the spot to which they have been accustomed. Where it is practicable, therefore, it is best to unite adjoining families; or when the union is to consist of three, unite to a hive in the centre, one on each side. A little foresight at the time of swarming, in the arrangement of the hives, will often facilitate after proceedings. Some have resorted to the plan of confinement of the bees, but this does not always meet the difficulty; for, on the first opportunity, many of them will return to their old haunts, and seek in vain their former dwelling.

Fumigation may often be resorted to in cases where a superabundance of honey exists in a hive at this season; for after the introduction of a little smoke the bees will fall down. It may then be reversed, and a portion of comb cut away in due moderation. Restore the bees to the hive, and replace its board, when the whole may be turned back to its proper position without injury.

Under the head of *Common Straw Hives*, we have remarked that suffocation with brimstone is the usual mode of obtaining possession of their stores; the stocks of the second or third year's standing being commonly selected for destruction. If, however, such stocks can be made strong and healthy in the way we have been detailing, good policy would point to the colonies of the present year as those affording the richest harvest of honey, and of the best quality, as being in new combs. These will never be of more value for the market than in the first autumn, provided the proprietor is satisfied as to the state of his older stocks for the next year's swarming. Such of the latter, moreover, as have sent out swarms in the same season will of course possess young Queens. In some districts this principle is carried out in practice, and doubtless with advantage, when a proper discretion is used. Under any circumstances, it is clear that in gaining possession of the honey, destruction of the bees may be avoided by adopting the fuming and uniting plan, instead of that of suffocation; for whether the hive be new or old, rich or poor, the same principle applies, with no amount of time, trouble, or expense, greater than under the brimstone system. The plea of necessity no longer exists for a wanton waste of valuable life; and to this point the attention of the cottager, in particular, might surely be directed, as one often involving his future profits. Let him know that it is his interest not to *kill his bees*; but, when expelled from one hive, to unite them to another, where augmented numbers will require no more than the usual stock of winter food. Inform him that he is acting on a mistaken principle when he imagines that his bees are worn out with age—the common plea for destroying them: that these are short-lived, and periodically renewed, so that the *hive* alone becomes old: moreover, that a large proportion of the bees at the close of the season are those produced in the later months; the older ones gradually disappearing in the autumn, to be succeeded by others destined to become the early labourers of the opening new year.[V]

[V] In a case where a proprietor had been obstinately bent on resorting to the old mode of destruction, the bees were stupefied by a wiser neighbour; taken home by him, and added to one of his own weak stocks, which turned to good account in the following spring.

Before we leave this part of our subject, a word may be said to those who are disposed to fancy there may be an evil in a super-abundant winter population in a hive. I never observed any permanent inconvenience arising from this; and no doubt can exist as to the advantage of maintaining a comfortable temperature, the Queen continuing to lay later in the autumn under such stimulant. Moreover, it must not be imagined that all the bees collected together to form a stock, at this time, are destined to survive till the spring. The day of life may, with many of them, be already far spent; but we have shown in what way their presence, though but temporary in the hive, indirectly contributes to augment the numbers of future spring labourers. Were it not so, there would be nothing to mark the well-known distinction between a populous and a half-tenanted hive. It is certain that, however numerous may be the eggs laid in the spring, a portion only are of avail in any but a hive so well peopled as to create a favorable temperature for hatching them, and to supply the means necessary to their full development. Thus strength in one year begets it in succeeding ones; and it must be remembered how influential is warmth to the early productive powers of the Queen, without which all goes wrong; and how important it is in the opening spring to be able to spare from the home duties of the hive a large number of collectors to add to the stores, which would otherwise not keep pace with the cravings of the rising generation.

Following up the principle thus laid down, I entirely agree with those who carry it out still further, by never destroying, if it can be avoided, the brood often found in quantity in a hive treated in the way we have been advising; for it is obvious that the latest hatched bees are those most likely to be of use in the spring. Where it is practicable, therefore, those combs which contain brood should, with as little loss of time as possible, to avoid chill, be arranged in a natural position, in a well-covered super, and placed over a hive requiring to be strengthened. The bees from below will ascend and cluster upon them and, in due time, a valuable accession of numbers will result. A deprived bar-hive offers many facilities in such cases, without injuring the combs.

It may not be misplaced here to remark, that, in the language of apiculturists, the hives of the year, *made up*, as it is termed, for the winter, now assume the name of *stocks*. Hitherto they have been denominated swarms or colonies. At this time a good selection of stocks may be made by those about to establish an apiary, to be removed at Christmas. In addition to the usual characteristics of vigour, such families are to be preferred as exhibit a certain degree of irascibility, for this is often most observable where there is most to defend.

Driving of Bees.—In the preceding section we have detailed the modes in practice for uniting bees, and for obtaining possession of their honey, by the aid of _fumigation_. Many proprietors, however, prefer to arrive at the same object by resorting to what is termed _Driving_; by which process the inmates of one hive are impelled to abandon it, and enter some other. When skilfully performed, this operation is often successful in attaining the end in view; but it is seldom well to attempt it, except in a pretty full hive. Mr. Golding has given, in a small compass, general directions as to the mode of procedure in common cases of Driving, and we will, therefore, adopt his words. "Towards dusk, when the family will be all at home, let the hive be raised gently from its floor-board, and supported on wedges about half an inch thick. When the bees shall have quietly ascended from the floor up into the hive, it may be inverted steadily on a small tub or pail. An empty hive, of the same diameter, being at hand, should be quickly set over the one turned up to receive it. A lighted pipe may be ready to give a puff or two if necessary, but the operation can generally be effected without using it. Tie a cloth firmly round the junction of the hives so that the bees cannot escape. Proceed to drum upon the full hive (opposite the sides of the combs, so as not to detach them), with the open hands or a couple of sticks; the bees will be so alarmed that in a few minutes they will have ascended into the hive set over them. A hive full of combs, and well peopled, always drives better than a weak and partly-filled one. The operation should never be attempted excepting in warm weather. If the object be to furnish another hive with the bees, there is nothing to do but to reverse the hive in which they are, and place the other upon it, again tying the cloth round the junction. A few raps upon the peopled hive will cause them to ascend, and early next morning they should be placed upon their usual stand. Those who still adhere to the common cottage hive may, by driving, deprive well-stored families of part of their honey. Having previously weighed the hive, calculate how much may be taken with safety, and cut away the external combs accordingly. The bees may then be returned as directed." Some operators vary the above proceeding, and perhaps diminish the danger, by placing, as the first step, the empty hive at the bottom, and the full one gently upon this. After making the junction complete between them, the two hives are reversed carefully together, so that the unoccupied one comes to the top, and the drumming then proceeds. This should be continued from five to ten minutes, according as circumstances indicate its necessity.

There are diversified ways of uniting the bees after they have been driven into an empty hive. Dr. Dunbar says, "turn up the stock-hive which is to receive the addition to its population: with a bunch of feathers, or a very small watering-pot, drench them with a solution of ale and sugar, or water and sugar, made a little warm. Do the same to the expelled bees: then placing these last over the stock, mouth to mouth, a rap on the top of the hive will drive them down among the bees and combs of the underneath hive. Place this last on its pedestal, and the operation is completed. The strong flavour of the solution will prevent the bees from distinguishing between friend and stranger."

Payne advocates the middle of a fine day as the best time for driving; removing the hive to be operated upon to a shady place, and then inverting over it an empty hive, as already described. A little smoke might sometimes be needful. Having ascertained that the bees have gone into the upper hive, Payne continues, "take the latter immediately to the place where the driven hive was taken from, and place it upon the same floor-board. Carry the driven hive fifty or sixty yards away; the few bees that remain in it, as well as those that are out at work, will return to the other hive, at the accustomed spot. All is now finished until an hour after sunset (excepting emptying the driven hive of its store), when two sticks may be laid upon the ground, about nine inches apart, opposite the stock-hive to which the driven bees are to be joined; then with a smart stroke dash out the bees between the sticks; and instantly, but gently, place the stock-hive over them upon the sticks: leave them for the night, protecting them from the weather, and an hour before sunrise restore the stock-hive to its original position. Here will be an increased population, enabled to stand through the winter much better, and to send out an earlier swarm, than if the union had not been effected."

The autumnal driving of bees is a common practice when the proprietors reside within a few miles of the moors and heaths, to which the hives are conveyed in time to luxuriate in a second harvest of blossom, now available from the heather. In such districts, it is not unusual to appropriate the whole contents of the driven hive; the bees being compelled to begin the world again in a new house and locality, like a recent swarm. Or, two or three small families may be driven into one. In a good season, a few weeks suffice to enable them to fill their second dwelling with combs, brood, and honey of the very finest quality. On their return home from the moors, some of the hives are again driven, and deprived of a portion of their stores; or united in many instances two or three together, to form strong families as stocks; for the value of population is too well understood to allow of any unnecessary destruction of life.

WINTER MANAGEMENT.

The management of bees in the winter season is probably that which is less understood than any other department of the apiary, and various have been the modes urged for ensuring safety through its various dangers. It seems, however, to be pretty generally admitted that it is better to allow the hives to remain in their usual position throughout the year; and our care therefore should be directed to ward off the casualties now to be guarded against. Ignorant attention, nevertheless, is sometimes worse even than neglect; and having once made the needful winter arrangements, there ought to be as little subsequent disturbance as possible. The great points to be observed are, adequate exterior covering and complete protection from the effects of wind, wet, and sudden changes of weather; a sufficiency of food to last till the spring; and preservation from damp in the hive, with its attendant evils. As regards the store of honey, we have already said that this is a matter to be clearly ascertained and supplied in autumn. When, therefore, as the cold weather sets in, and the bees have collected and clustered together, there must be no more attempts at feeding. The mouth of the hive should gradually be contracted, as the winter advances, though never entirely closed. After every fall of snow, let it be cleared away from the hives, and about the stand or house, to prevent the chance of reflection, which always injuriously arouses the bees, and for the better security from moist exhalation on thawing.

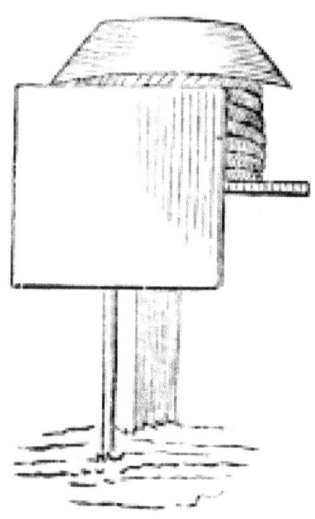

Winter position.—It is extremely desirable in winter to keep off the influence of the sun from the front of the hives. Some persons recommend moving them from their summer position to a north aspect, or turning them round on their stands. But this shifting of quarters involves the necessity of shutting up the bees close prisoners till the spring; for all that casually left the hive would fly back to the original familiar spot, never more to revisit home. I entirely agree with those who assert that bees are never healthy where confinement has been long continued. "Who shuts up the wild bees in the forests of Lithuania, where they thrive so well?" asks Gelieu. Surely in this, as in other parts of our practice, we cannot do better than follow the guidance of nature. On a fine day, with the thermometer at or not much below 50° (and these are not of unfrequent occurrence in winter), the bees avail themselves of it, sallying forth in evident delight, with certain advantage to health and cleanliness; for they void nothing in the hive, unless compelled by long necessity. This is the point at which disease commences: indeed the retention of their fæces sometimes occasions death. Their impatience of confinement is excessive, and increases as the season advances, so that they will leave the hive at a lower temperature after Christmas than before. But in thus advocating the principle of liberty, I am not insensible to the evil it may bring with it, if not guarded against. The most disastrous consequences follow the flight of bees on a frosty day, when the gleams and deceitful warmth of a winter sun reach their domicile, particularly with snow on the ground, the glare of which allures them out to destruction, for they soon fall down to rise no more. The remedy for this is the screening of the hive in some way from its effects; and it should be done as soon as winter actually sets in. At the same time it is important that no obstruction to the free passage of air is presented, or dysentery among the bees would be the certain consequence. Where the hives stand singly, I have always seen the advantage of fixing before each a wooden screen, nailed to a post, sunk in the ground, and large enough to throw the whole front into shade. This does not interfere with the coming forth of the bees at a proper temperature; and it supersedes any necessity for shutting them up when snow is on the ground. The screen should be fixed a foot or two in advance, and so as to intercept the sun's rays, which will be chiefly in winter towards the west side. Other plans have been tried for effecting the same object, such as blocks placed at the mouth of the hive; but these answer no good end, as the rays of light penetrate underneath and around them. In a bee-house, entirely enclosed at the front, the hives and their boards may sometimes at this season be advantageously shifted a little sideways of the exterior entrance way; with hollowed blocks (see page 96), shaped in accordance, to intercept the light, but not the air.

A screen of the kind we have described has the further tendency to promote the security of the bees, where other enemies than wind, frost, snow, or sun might sometimes endanger them. One of these, at this time, is the blue Titmouse, to which we have before alluded. Old Purchas says, "She will eat ten or twelve bees at a time, and by-and-by be ready for more. When she cometh to the hive and findeth none, she knocketh with her bill at the door, and as soon as the bees come out to inquire the cause, she catcheth first one and then another, until her belly be full." At page 117 we have described a mode of dealing with these marauders.

Damp in Hives.—Perhaps there is nothing more prejudicial than the moisture often engendered in exposed hives at this time, particularly after frost, and in certain states of the atmosphere. It accumulates on the top and sides, moulding and rendering offensive the combs, and producing disease amongst the bees. For this reason, hives with flat roofs have sometimes been objected to; and perhaps justly, where no provision is made for ventilation. Gelieu obviated the evil by placing caps or small hives (cemented down) over the stocks; the moisture ascending, evaporated through the opening, "as by a chimney," I have tried different experiments, and have found nothing better than the practice of condensing the vapour of the hive as much as possible, and conveying it away. At the beginning of winter, over the hole on the top, a piece of perforated zinc or wood is placed. Upon this let one of the common feeding troughs, already described, be put, from which the glass cover, and, if you please, the perforated bottom, are previously removed; the hole in the pan being placed over the one below. This may be covered with a bell-glass, standing within the pan. As the exhalation rises from the bees below, it is condensed on the glass, and received, often in considerable quantity, in the pan. The hole at the top of the glass may be stopped, opening it occasionally on a fine day, to allow the escape of vitiated air. The change of air in a hive, in mild, dry weather, is always conducive to health, till the early spring breeding begins, when caution against chill to the bees is needed. In the absence of a bell-glass, the glass cover to the trough may be kept in its place as a substitute. We have already recommended the giving to all hives or boxes a slight inclination forwards, as being useful in conveying away the moisture.

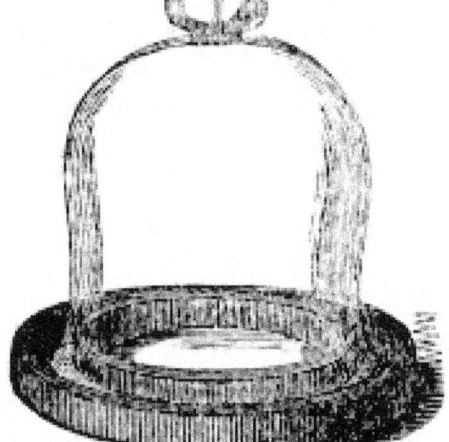

Where there is no feeding pan, a bell-glass may be put within a circular leaden or zinc trough, having the centre open, and placed over the hole below.

Temperature.—With good protection from cutting winds, from wet without, and from damp within, the effects of cold alone, unless of extreme severity, need not be apprehended, for the bees of a strong stock will generate sufficient warmth; and a dry season is often better sustained than a mild, moist one. It is of importance to guard against *sudden changes* of temperature, often occurring in winter; and experienced bee-keepers have recommended covering each hive with a mat, or something of the kind, as a regulator.

It is certain that less food is consumed at a low than a high temperature, and that the bees are often healthy in proportion. I have known the thermometer down to 32° in a box, with no bad effect to the bees when *clustered together*; but they would become torpid if exposed *singly* to this, or to a much less degree of cold, especially towards the close of winter; and could then only be recovered by artificial warmth.[W] The action of very severe frost, moreover, has an injurious effect upon the honey, which becomes candied at the extremities of the combs, and sometimes throughout. It is thenceforth useless as food for the bees.[X]

[W] It is frequently the case in winter that a number of bees may be found, apparently dead, about a hive, particularly after sudden disturbance. The greater part of these are merely paralysed on coming out into a lower temperature, and may be recovered by taking them to the fire. But this should be done with caution; for, if placed too near, the bees are not so likely permanently to recover, as when the restoration is gradual. The best way is to put the bees into a large basin, spreading over it a piece of muslin to confine them till they are restored to the hive.

[X] In two stocks which I had an opportunity of examining, at the end of February, 1838, after a very severe winter, I found cells filled with honey in a granulated state, and perfectly white. This was untouched by the bees, though distressed for food. Notwithstanding the unusual severity of the season, there was brood in various stages of progression.

A thermometer is not always a criterion of the state of the hive at this season, as I have often found; for the temperature varies as the bees recede from it, and they frequently shift their quarters, moving in a mass to preserve the warmth. When congregated immediately about the thermometer, I have known it rise as much as 30° on a frosty day; and an increase of temperature always follows any commotion, from whatever cause, or partial activity in the dwelling, resulting in an increased consumption of food.

Dysentery.—Care should be taken to clear away any dead bees at the mouth of the hive, for these give great offence, besides endangering the safety of the family, by preventing the passage of air. Whilst the bees are in activity, they carefully remove every dead body from the hive; but in winter this service should be occasionally performed for them. In particular it should be attended to if signs of dysentery appear, which may be known by the dark-coloured evacuations, offensive smell in the hive, and frequent deaths. This malady often attacks the strongest hives, too much closed at the mouth, particularly at the latter part of winter or in early spring, the most critical time for bees; and no doubt it is attributable to unnaturally retained fæces in a damp impure atmosphere, with deficient covering and ventilation. It has been thought that the want of water predisposes the bees to dysentery. As soon as the disease is apparent, no time should be lost in lifting the hive from its board, expelling the vitiated air, and scraping and washing away all impurity; repeating the same process, if requisite, on some fine subsequent day. But the board should be dried before the hive is replaced on it; or a fresh one may be at once substituted for it, with less loss of time and annoyance to the bees. I have restored a stock to perfect health by thoroughly cleaning and ventilating it, after a third of the inhabitants had fallen a sacrifice. All remedies, as they are called, by feeding with various prescriptions, do more harm than good. "Bees," says Gelieu, "have no real disease: dysentery, about which so much noise has been made, and for which so many remedies have been prescribed, never attacks the bees of a well-stocked hive that is left open at all seasons, but only those that are too long and too closely confined. They are always in good health as long as they are at liberty; when they are warm enough and have plenty of food. All their pretended diseases are the result of cold, hunger, or the infection produced by a too close and long confinement during the winter."

SPRING MANAGEMENT.

Those who commence an apiary by the purchase of established stock-hives, and who did not secure such in the autumn, can, with the opening of February, and for the five or six weeks ensuing, make a selection of those that have the characteristics of health and strength, which may generally be ascertained on a fine day, by observing the quantity of farina carried into a hive. "The best time," says Payne, "to establish an apiary is from the middle of February to the middle of March. The stocks will have passed through the winter, and the removal is safe and easy. There are few commodities in which a person can be so easily deceived as in a hive of bees. I would, therefore, recommend the young apiarian to take the opinion of some experienced person before he makes his purchase. If the hive is not of the preceding year, its weight is no criterion of its value; for an old stock contains a large quantity of pollen." An examination of the combs, as to discoloration, will often be a useful criterion of age. The selected stocks should be removed to their new quarters by hand, at dusk, to be no more disturbed.

Cleaning or changing Floor-boards.—All who have been accustomed to the care of bees must have perceived the saving of labour to them, in the early spring, in the cleaning of their floor-boards, by scraping away all filth, removing dead bees, refuse wax, &c., and thoroughly drying them. In many cases the best and quickest plan is to change the board, and particularly when it shows signs of decay, which always leads to mischief.

Comb-pruning.—In conjunction with an examination of the floor-boards, opportunity can be taken of observing the state of the hives, as respects their combs. Where these are seen to be old, mouldy, mildewed, or infected by moths, they should be cut away; as also when they have become filled with a mass of stale pollen and useless honey; at the same time taking care not to disturb any brood there may be. Hives sometimes contain too large a proportion of drone-combs, which can now be removed with advantage. Some persons use a little smoke, but at this season it must be resorted to sparingly, as the bees are weak. They will speedily fill up the vacancies thus made, and a stock in this way partially renewed may be continued in health several years, provided the hive itself is in good state. Nevertheless, it may be well to recur to an opinion we have already expressed, that it is often more to the interest of the proprietor to allow a stock to swarm rather than to persevere for several succeeding seasons in preventing it, in a hive constantly becoming worse for occupation.

General directions.—As soon as vegetation begins to appear, with genial weather, all obstructions to the free access to the hives must be removed; and by degrees extended space given at the mouth. The critical time for the bees is now approaching; for in February brood often rapidly increases, requiring greater attention to a uniform warmth. The tops of the hives, therefore, should be closed in, to prevent currents of cold air, often at this time fatal both to the eggs and larvæ, as may be seen by the ejectment of dead grubs. Even much later on in the season the recurrence of cold days will leave certain proofs of mischief; and at such times the mouths of the hives ought again to be contracted and screened; carefully retaining till all danger is past the outer coverings to the hives.

The bees will now, in fine weather, go forth in search of pollen, which they bring into the hive in large or apparently in useless quantity, so as sometimes to render it necessary afterwards to remove it, at a great expense of labour. "This," says Gelieu, "is the only point on which they can be accused of a want of that prudence and foresight, so admirable in every other respect." A supply of pollen, together with water, are the first requirements of the spring, both essential to the brood, and the eagerness of the bees to seek them is a certain indication of health and strength in the hive.[Y] At page 102, a list is given of early flowering plants, which it is desirable to have in the immediate vicinity of the hives. At present the bees are weak, and incapable of a long flight: the weather, too, is often unfavorable for it.

[Y] It is worthy of attention that a distinguished German apiculturist has recently introduced a substitute for pollen in the early year, when the bees have no means of procuring it. Observing that his bees frequented a neighbouring mill, he found them engaged in conveying from thence a quantity of rye meal. Deriving a hint from this discovery, he placed a trough of the meal in front of his apiary, which was eagerly carried to the hives, the bees preferring it to old pollen; and this continued till the opening blossoms supplied the natural article. Some hives consumed as much as two pounds. Subsequent experimentalists, at home, have used the flour of wheat, or other grain, with success. The knowledge that the collection of pollen and the need of water by the bees are simultaneous, led these observers a step further, by giving a supply of both these essentials at the same time. As this assistance has been afforded as early as January, it would seem necessary, in our climate, to place both articles in some accessible part within the hive. In the absence of any better provision, wet sponge or moss has been found to answer; or old combs will suffice as receptacles either of water or flour. Stocks thus treated are said to be greatly forwarded both in breeding and swarming.

An attentive observer will now readily distinguish the strong, healthy stocks; but now and then a family may be seen sluggish in its work, though, perhaps, not deficient in numbers. The cause may generally be traced to an unfruitful Queen, to be got rid of as soon as the season is a little more advanced, and a successor can be reared in the way described under the head *Queen Bee*. Or, it might happen if the Queen dies before the bees have the means of establishing another, when an abandonment of the hive often ensues, though honey may still be plentiful in store. Prudence will at this time point out the expediency of surveying the state of the apiary as to repairs, painting, &c., to be done before the bees have fully entered into a state of activity.

Spring-feeding.—It is well now to examine the remaining stock of food, for much will shortly be required for the increasing numbers. If needed, some must be given, though in less quantity than in autumn; and it ought to be placed within the hive, either at the top or bottom; but the time is arrived when every precaution should be used to prevent the effects of chill to the brood, by the creation of cold currents. It usually suffices to supply food about three times a week, but the feeding trough must be closely covered, to keep up the temperature, or the bees will not at first enter into it. When this is the case, some proprietors do not hesitate to invert a hive, and pour a cup of honey amongst the combs: the bees will soon lick one another clean. Or, in lieu of a trough, I have used a tin vessel, holding nearly half a pint, open at each end, made somewhat taper downwards, the lower end fitting into a hole on the top of the hive, of about two inches. This part is somewhat loosely tied over with linen cloth, through which the bees suck the food. It may be made cylindrical, if preferred, with a flanch to rest upon. At this season it is well to give the food slightly warmed. Many persons recommend feeding even the strong hives, for it is certain the bees are stimulated by the increased temperature to which it gives rise; and there can be no doubt of the importance of bringing the stocks forward as early as possible. But no feeding, unless from absolute necessity, should be resorted to till a certain degree of animation is visible in the dwelling, otherwise the bees are prematurely put in motion, and numbers perish, unable to reach home. Nor is it of less importance to observe that feeding is not discontinued too soon; for even after warm days there will be a return of ungenial weather, and a stock might perish where a very little additional food would have saved it. But some limit should be put to the quantity as the weather becomes fine and warm; for I have known evil arise where the cells have been filled by the bees with sugared mixtures, at the time when the Queen requires them to deposit eggs. We have already alluded to the advantages of a supply of water withinside, in the very early year, before the bees can go abroad.

Where honey is abundant, it is of course preferable; and it is no worse for being slightly made liquid with water. In other cases various kinds of substitutes have been resorted to. I have used good sound ale, sweetened with sugar and honey, and boiled for a minute or two: the usual proportion is a pint to a pound of refined sugar, adding a fourth part of pure honey, which imparts a flavour the most agreeable to the bees. A tablespoonful of rum still further improves the compound. Mr. Golding recommends a very similar mixture; to which, however, he adds a teaspoonful of salt and a glass of wine. Payne prescribes lump sugar, in the proportion of three pounds to a pint of water, boiled for two or three minutes, and mixed with a pound of honey.

The kind of food we have been describing is that which is most commonly used for bees at this season. I have, however, turned my attention, occasionally, to the saving of trouble that arises where food can be given them in a concrete form, to supersede some of the evils attending the common methods of administering liquids at this season. In one of my feeding troughs I have sometimes put some large lumps of refined sugar, dipped previously in water till pretty well saturated, which the bees will appropriate. Of the various concrete saccharine preparations, however, I have found none entirely combining the needful requisites except that in which the crystallizing properties of the sugar had been altogether destroyed. It is well known that this change can be effected by certain methods of boiling. I believe I am correct in stating that the heat required to convert crystallizable into uncrystallizable sugar is from 320° to 360° of Fahrenheit. If, therefore, to two pounds of loaf sugar half a pint of water is added in a saucepan, it must be boiled up to a temperature not exceeding 360° of heat. This may be pretty well known when the syrup becomes brittle; ascertainable by suddenly cooling a little on a cold substance, or plate, when it begins to assume a pale yellow colour. The longer it is exposed to heat, up to this point, the more perfect is the change produced; but about twenty minutes' boiling is usually sufficient. If, instead of water alone, a fifth to a fourth part of vinegar is mixed with it, the process is expedited; and when thus made, the bees appear to give it a preference. The whole must be poured out gradually upon a cold dish, or a slab of stone, marble, or slate, previously rubbed with a very little fine oil, or other unctuous matter, to prevent adhesion. In a few minutes it is sufficiently stiffened to allow of being cut, with a pair of scissors, into such conveniently-formed pieces as are best adapted for insertion into the hive at its mouth. To those who do not object to the trouble of preparing this kind of bee-food themselves, the cost may be estimated at that of the sugar, as there does not appear to arise any loss in weight. It will be seen that this preparation differs but little from the common confection, familiarly known as barley-sugar. The bees, as lambent insects, have no difficulty, from the deliquescent properties of this concrete, in appropriating it speedily; and in the use of a large quantity I have always found it to be unaccompanied by the usual degree of disturbance, observable when honey is administered. It may be given at any time of the day; and an impoverished family might frequently be saved by inserting a few sticks of barley-sugar within a hive, when any other mode of feeding was impracticable. In fact it would appear that no other artificial food is so acceptable to the bees;

and much of it doubtless returns to the proprietor, intermixed with natural honey. By the process we have described, common sugar has now been converted into a substance much resembling in its properties the saccharine matter of certain fruits, as grapes, &c., known as uncrystallizable sugar; probably nearly identical with the honey collected by the bees from the nectaries of flowering plants. After exposure to the action of a moist atmosphere, the concrete soon assumes a dissolved form; and so, thenceforth, remains, as I have proved by keeping it, in any way unaltered, for several years; in short, it becomes a substance very much resembling honey.[Z]

[Z] I am not amongst the number of those who (to my apprehension) go out of their way to maintain that this vegetable secretion undergoes some kind of chemical change by passing into the stomach of the bees (in reality a mere receiving bag), from whence it is often regurgitated into the cells of the combs in a few minutes, or even seconds, of time. Honey doubtless derives both its colour and flavour immediately from the plants supplying it; the bees not possessing the power of altering either. It even sometimes contains an original poisonous matter. Its subsequent thickened consistency naturally results from the effect of a lowered temperature; acting in a greater or less degree, according to circumstances, season, &c. That the bees have not the ability to change chemically the contents received into their honey-bags, is shown by an examination of the saccharine mixtures given to them as artificial food; in which I never could detect any alteration after being stored in the combs.

Enemies and robbers.—The enemies of bees, already pointed out at p. 116, should now have the attention of the proprietor; and more especially robber-bees, for these are sometimes troublesome at this season, particularly where the hives are placed not sufficiently apart. Let a vigilant look-out be given for Queen-wasps, now becoming common, and destroy them in any way possible; remembering that each of these is the parent of a future family. When the wasps are seen to alight, the use of a garden syringe and water is often effectual in disabling them from flying, when they are easily killed.

Super-hives.—As the season continues to open, young bees will become numerous, timidly peeping out of the hive, and distinguishable by the lightness of their colour. With genial weather, wealth also rapidly accumulates; and the strong odour of the hive, and increased activity of its inmates, attest the growing prosperity of the family. Attention now is requisite to these symptoms of a rising temperature, and, consequently, to the crowding of the hive. If the glass windows become sensibly warm, attended with clustering at the mouth, increased building room should at once be given, or under the head of *Nadiring stocks*; for a fertile Queen will require a large proportion of the stock-hive for the purpose of depositing eggs. Should a few cold nights ensue, the supers must be kept covered; and more especially glasses, which the bees will desert unless a warm temperature is fully preserved in them.

I much doubt the probability of preventing the swarming of bees, where the extra storing room is delayed till royal cells have become tenanted, or, perhaps, only formed. Mischief has also frequently arisen where the bees have all at once had a large additional space given them of too cold a temperature; and often rendered more unacceptable by undue or ill-timed ventilation, as in using Nutt's hives was often the case. The same cause has sometimes operated to prevent progress of any kind; and in a collateral hive, thus managed, I witnessed the fact that, during five or six successive seasons, there was no more breeding or storing than barely sufficed to keep the unhappy family in existence, the proprietor deriving no benefit whatever.

Temperature and weather.—With the advance of the season, and a more abundant efflorescence, the buzz of the hive becomes louder and more general, and particularly when the family are all assembled at night. And now the exertions of the bees are called into action for the purpose of promoting ventilation, and expelling the vitiated air. This they accomplish by means of a rapid and continuous fanning, or vibration of their wings, giving rise collectively to the sound usually termed *humming*; and which is readily distinguishable from the sharp, angry note emitted by a bee under the excitement of irritation. Sometimes the heat of the hives impels the inhabitants to seek a cooler temperature by clustering on the outside. At such times it is often well to aid in moderating the warmth by slightly raising up the bottom edge of the supers with a few strips of wood or lead. At p. 115, we have given some general recommendations relative to the shading of exposed hives, now to be attended to; as also on the subject of water.

In most localities, the best part of the honey season will now be approaching; and much consequently depends on the state of the weather. In particular, a prevalence of dry easterly winds, acting on vegetation, causes the suspension of almost all operations; so that the main honey-storing time is often limited to three or four weeks in the season, or frequently even less, in our uncertain climate. The secretion of honey is remarkably promoted by an electric state of the atmosphere. Huber says truly of the bees: "I have remarked that the collection by these creatures is never more abundant, nor their operations in wax more active, than when the wind is from the south, the air moist and warm, and a storm approaching." A certain commencement of the latter is to be looked for when the bees are seen rapidly hurrying home in crowds to the hive. Payne may be cited in this connexion. "I am not aware," he observes, "that bees have ever been placed in the list of those animals which are said to foretell the changes of weather, as many of the feathered and insect tribes are; but in my opinion they stand foremost of the weather-wise. A nice observer, by looking at them in the early morning during the working season, will very soon be able to form an opinion as to what the day will be, and that almost to a certainty; for they will sometimes appear sluggish and inactive, although the morning is very bright, and showing every appearance for a fine day; but the sun soon becomes clouded, and rain follows. And, again, the morning may be dull and cloudy, and sometimes rain may be falling; still the bees will be observed going out in considerable numbers; and as sure as this is seen the day becomes bright and fair."

"Thou wert out betimes, thou busy, busy bee! When abroad I took my early way: Before the cow from her resting-place Had risen up, and left her trace On the meadow, with dew so gray, I saw thee, thou busy, busy bee! Thou wert alive, thou busy, busy bee! When the crowd in their sleep were dead Thou wert abroad in the freshest hour, When the sweetest odour comes from the flower; Man will not learn to leave his lifeless bed, And be wise, and copy thee, thou busy, busy bee! Thou wert working late, thou busy, busy bee! After the fall of the cistus flower; I heard thee last as I saw thee first, When the primrose free blossom was ready to burst; In the coolness of the evening hour, I heard thee, thou busy, busy bee!"   Southey.

Swarming.—The month of May, in fine seasons, usually brings with it the period of the greatest interest to the proprietor, as regards the swarming stocks of bees; on which subject we would refer to p. 21. Drones now begin to make their appearance, darting out of the hive in the middle of warm days, though occasionally in strong stocks they may be seen in April; in which event early swarming may be looked for. The usual limits during which swarming takes place vary in different localities; but in general they are comprised in the months of May and June; though in extraordinary circumstances a swarm may issue somewhat earlier, or a little later than this. When it is expected, the hive should be watched from ten in the morning till two or three o'clock, after which time swarming rarely occurs. In particular, the bees ought not to be left for five minutes if a hot sun intervene between showers; for a greater predisposition to swarming then exists than in dry weather; it seldom, however, takes place with an east or north wind.

It is not always easy to distinguish the appearances that precede a first (or *prime*) swarm, and experienced apiculturists are sometimes deceived. If, however, we had access to the interior of the hive, the usual time would always be found (accidents as to weather not interfering) to be that in which the larvæ of the royal cells were about to be transformed into nymphs, and therein sealed up; viz., eight or nine days before the young Queens are matured; for it is to be remembered that on the occasion of a first swarm it is always the *old* Queen that accompanies it. The issue of a swarm is frequently to be expected when the bees have remained for some time previously in a state of seeming inertness, followed by an unusual commotion among the drones; and more especially if these make their appearance in the morning, hanging out with a cluster of bees; conjointly with a disinclination to foraging abroad, among the workers. If, in addition, the honey previously stored in a super is observed to disappear suddenly, swarming may be anticipated, as the bees load themselves before leaving home. But mere clustering at the mouth of the hive is not invariably the precursor of a swarm; and the bees frequently continue to congregate in unmeaning idleness on the outside, even though honey may be abundant. "In this case," says Dr. Bevan, "the cluster may be swept into an empty hive towards dusk, and carried to a short distance from the apiary, when they will gradually return, and generally join the family." This, however, is often only a temporary expedient; and the prolonged continuance of a period of inaction frequently denotes the absence, from abortion, or other cause, of a young Queen; the old one not choosing to leave the hive without the prospect of a successor. Or it may be that the hive contains an unfruitful Queen, and a weak population with insufficient warmth, when little of store is collected, and often no drone eggs are produced, these being always the preliminary of royal cells. A continuation of unfavorable weather, moreover, notwithstanding the sealing up of the Queen-cells, will often prevent any issue of a swarm; for the reigning sovereign will avail herself of this compulsory detention in severally destroying the young princesses as they are matured. An old Queen is permitted by the bees to do this, but it is otherwise with a young one, till a later stage. Neither as to swarming will the state of the thermometer be an invariable guide. I have rarely seen it reach as high as 95° within a stock-hive, but I have observed the issue of swarms at a temperature four or five degrees below this; and in one instance it occurred when the thermometer ranged but little above 80°.[AA]

[AA] Some naturalists, and amongst them Huber, have imagined a much higher degree of heat at the time of swarming; but in this there must be some error, for I have proved that the combs collapse and fall at a temperature a little above 100°. I am almost ashamed to say that this experiment cost me the destruction of a fine stock-hive.

It is common to imagine that a swarm consists exclusively of the young bees of the season; but Nature is no such bungler, or what would become of the parent stock? Accordingly, we find that bees of all ages, and usually several hundreds of drones, go forth intermingled, to form the new family. It is not always an easy matter to estimate the strength of a swarm. The bulk is not entirely a criterion, as the temperature of the weather causes the bees to cluster together more or less closely. A pint will usually contain about 2000. Five thousand bees are estimated to weigh nearly a pound; but this also varies, for on swarming they are always provident enough to load themselves more or less with honey before their departure. A good swarm, however, ought to weigh about four pounds. Some have reached to six pounds, but this is rare.

Returning of swarms.—Cases sometimes occur in which it is thought desirable to compel the return of a swarm to the stock-hive. On this subject we will use the words of Payne. "The process," says he, "is very simple, and I have always found it succeed. As soon as the swarm is settled in the hive, turn it bottom upwards, and, if the Queen-bee does not make her appearance in a few seconds, dash the bees out upon a cloth, or a gravel walk, and with a wine-glass she may be easily captured. Upon this the bees will return to their parent hive. The queen may also very easily be taken during the departure of a swarm; for she appears to leave the hive reluctantly, and may be seen running backwards and forwards upon the alighting-board before she takes wing." I have sometimes found it advantageous, instead of a cloth, to place on the ground four or five sheets of large paper. On these the bees have been spread, and the sheets carried in opposite directions, thus enabling a better search to be made for the Queen; and especially in the case of a second swarm, for then there are frequently three or four. Where there is no Queen, the bees will soon be in confusion and fly to their original home; but in the reverse case, she may be discovered by their congregating in one particular part. Nor is there any danger in thus proceeding; for the bees, being gorged with honey, are not often disposed to attack, with the precaution of not breathing upon them. Moreover, any such operation is best done in the shade, as a hot sun makes the bees less tractable at all times. Occasionally it might happen that, on the issuing of a swarm, the Queen, from inability to fly, falls to the ground, when the bees will return to the hive, which is often attended with advantage.

In judging of the desirableness of compelling the return of a first swarm, we must be guided by circumstances. Should it be a large issue, expediency would dictate the hiving it at once, as a new colony; for the Queen may reasonably be supposed to be a vigorous one, and a compulsory returning of the bees to the parent hive (the result of destroying her) would occasion a loss of valuable time; a young Queen not yet being in a state to commence laying eggs. On the other hand, a poor swarm might denote an unfruitful Queen, to be got rid of in the way we have just pointed out. The bees would re-issue under a young sovereign, after the usual interval, with a large accession of numbers, the produce of the brood matured in the mean time; and this might have the further good effect of preventing an after-swarm, which is always desirable.

It has already been said that on the occasion of a first swarm the *old* Queen invariably issues with it. It is also a fact that she leaves no actual successor, but that an interregnum usually occurs of eight or nine days; the royal larva being left short of maturity by this period, unless bad weather has interposed to delay the issuing of the swarm, in which event this interval may be much shortened; it is also subject to extension under certain contingencies of weather. The first princess that is subsequently liberated from her cell becomes the future mistress of the hive, unless she leaves it with an after-issue; for the law of primogeniture has been observed to be strictly followed. It is therefore evident that no regal disagreement can occur except in the cases of after-swarms, when a Queen returning to the stock-hive might chance to find a rival, and would have to contest her way to the supremacy.

After-swarms.—It is not an unusual thing to hear a boast of a number of swarms from a stock-hive; but nothing is proved by this beyond the fact, that a thriving community has been weakened (if not destroyed) by too much subdivision. The proprietor, therefore, must not imagine that his care is ended with the return of a swarm to the parent hive. Though one Queen has been removed, several successors are usually at hand, and swarming may occur again and again, so long as more than one is left. The hive must be watched more especially from the eighth to about the twelfth day from the departure of a first swarm, after which another rarely issues; the probability, or rather the certainty, then being, that the first-liberated young Queen has succeeded in destroying the others—an event always to be desired. But the symptoms which precede a second issue are more unequivocal than those in the previous case. The young princesses are now arriving at maturity, and two or more may be ready to come forth at the same time; impatiently awaiting the assistance of the bees to liberate them from imprisonment; for, unlike the workers and drones, they are not allowed by their own volition to leave their cells. In this state of confinement they are objects of great solicitude, and are supplied with food through a small orifice in their cocoon, till one of them is set at liberty, which is never till she is able to fly. At this precise period, a singular and plaintive call or croak, proceeding from the young Queens, may be heard, often at a distance of several feet from the hive, and more particularly in the evening. These notes are of two kinds, according as the princesses emit them from without or within their cells. For want of a more distinctive term, these sounds have obtained the name of *piping*. To Huber we are largely indebted for the knowledge we possess as regards this peculiarity in the natural history of the bee; and his observations have since received abundant confirmation,—perhaps from no apiarian more satisfactorily than from Mr. Golding. "The first note of piping heard," says the latter, "is low and plaintive, and is uttered by the princess already *at liberty*, and I have frequently seen her emit it. She traverses the hive, stopping upon or near the royal cells which still contain brood, and emits her *long* plaintive note. This, when the other young Queens are sufficiently forward (generally in about two days), is answered by them from *within* their cells, in a quick, *short*, hoarse note. After these last have been heard for about two days, the swarm may be expected to come off." "These sounds, therefore," in the words of Keys, "convey to the apiarian one certain warning, that when heard, he may be assured the first or prime swarm has escaped." But universal as this rule has been considered, it has not been entirely without exception; for in a stock-hive of Dr. Bevan's, in the remarkable season of 1852, swarming had been so long prevented by bad weather, that a young Queen became liberated, and escaping into a super, piping was the consequence for two days before the issue of a *prime* swarm.

After-swarms are frequently accompanied by more than one young Queen; often by three or four, and always in the virgin state. "Indeed," observes Mr. Golding, "it would appear that all which are ready to quit their cells (one only, be it remembered, being at liberty in the hive, until the moment of swarming) go off with the swarm; leaving the more forward of the younger princesses to come off with subsequent swarms, or 'fight out' their title to the sovereignty of the parent stock at home."

A third and even a fourth issue sometimes takes place, the intervening periods successively becoming shorter, and more piping being heard. As all the royal cells must have been tenanted before the old Queen departed from the hive, it follows that from sixteen to eighteen days comprise the limit during which, under ordinary circumstances, swarming can occur; and thenceforth the Queen-bee is mute for the year. Moreover, the worker brood originally left in the hive will now, or in a few days, be matured, leaving the combs less occupied, probably in any way, than at any other period of the year, until the young reigning Queen is in a condition again to stock them with eggs. This state of the hive is therefore considered by some as the most favorable for examination and excision of old combs, and other operations usually attended to in the spring.

I have known piping after a second swarm has departed, where no third issue has followed. The second swarm, however, in this instance, was restored to the stock-hive on the same evening, together with one Queen. This is often the best time for making a reunion of after-swarms; for I have usually found that all the Queens except one are ejected on the day of swarming: she, being stronger than those still in the parent hive, is able to destroy them on her return to it. If a cloth is spread on a table, placed in front of the old hive, at dusk, the bees of the swarm can be jerked out upon it, and guided to its mouth. In two hours after the reunion just mentioned, piping from a Queen at liberty was heard. The next day two young Queens were ejected; one of them torn from its cell, not having attained its full growth. From the other the sting was protruding, evidently the result of a recent combat. Piping was again heard on the following morning; and soon after, another princess, doubtless the last, was cast out of the hive, which I took away still alive; making five in all, since the issue of the first swarm. We may observe that when swarming has taken place more than once, the original utilitarian principle no longer impels the bees to guard the royal cells; the reigning princess being then permitted to tear them open and destroy any prospective rival.

No point has been better established, than the fact recorded by Huber, as to the destruction of the supernumerary young Queens by their combating together; the sovereignty remaining with the single survivor. "In order," says Huber, "that at no time there may be a plurality of females in a hive, Nature has inspired Queens with an innate inveteracy against one another. They never meet without endeavouring to fight, and accomplish their mutual destruction. If one combatant is older than the rest, she is stronger, and the advantage will be with her. She will destroy her rivals successively as produced. Thence, if the old Queen did not leave the hive before the young ones undergo their last metamorphosis, it could produce no more swarms, and the species would perish."

It is not clear by what instinct bees are guided as respects after-swarms, or rather as to the construction of royal cells; for, as has been shown, these abound much more in some hives than in others. The repeated issues occasioned by the presence of supernumerary young Queens, although there has previously been a rapid development of brood, not only leaves a hive comparatively depopulated, but the succession of interregnums is mischievous as operating to suspend, not breeding alone, but almost entirely the gathering of honey. A different kind of instinct appears to direct the bees than is observable at the time of the original issue; for the young Queens will depart in weather that would be thought unfavorable for the issuing of an *old* one. "The reason seems evident," observes Mr. Golding; "for when the proper age of the young Princesses has arrived, the swarm must go off, or not at all, as the younger would be destroyed by the eldest." As a natural consequence, there is evidently less of foresight as regards the future place of abode. Where so much of prudence and seeming intelligence are discernible in all the proceedings of these wonderful insects, it is hardly to be expected that mere chance should direct on so important an occasion as the change of residence; although when a swarm suddenly finds itself in a comfortable dwelling, by the act of hiving, it is rarely inclined to relinquish it. A hive containing a few combs, placed in the season near an apiary, is almost certain to receive a colony, which will sometimes fly to it at once, without any previous clustering. [AB] The instances are numerous of prime swarms proceeding a considerable distance to a new domicile, carefully inspected and cleaned beforehand. I was an eye-witness to an example of this, where the bees, taking a dislike to the hive in which they had been housed, soon after quitted it; and, mounting high in the air, flew in a direct line to the roof of a church nearly a mile distant. But an after-swarm appears to have little or nothing of preparation; and has been known, in seeming perplexity, to commence comb-building in the bush on which it had alighted.

[AB] In the garden of a friend stood an untenanted hive, in which were a few empty combs. Some straggling strange bees were observed hovering about and in it, for several successive days; and, at my suggestion, the hive was left undisturbed. On the day following, a fine swarm of bees suddenly made its appearance, undoubtedly from a distance, and entered the hive. In this instance, a few hundreds, or perhaps dozens, of pioneers alone could have been in the secret as to the locality of the chosen domicile to which they so sagaciously conducted their Queen and a community of perhaps 20,000 bees.

Uniting of Swarms.—It has been shown that it is easy to compel the return of a swarm of bees to the parent hive; but their remaining there depends much upon accidental circumstances. We have seen that several young Queens are often only waiting their time and opportunity to leave their cells and depart from the hive; and till all these are in some way or other disposed of, there can be no progress made in the family. Under such circumstances, many persons think it best to hive all swarms in the usual way, and to strengthen the later ones by joining two or three of them together; for, separately, these are rarely of any value. In cases where more than one after-swarm or subdivided swarm, comes out on the same day, each can often with little difficulty be shaken into the same hive, at the time: or the branches on which such swarms cluster may be cut off, and brought to one hive. Otherwise, a generally certain method of union may be resorted to at night. At any time, within a few days after the first swarm has been established, another may be added to it. On the same evening of the issue, in front of the one to which it is to be joined, place a table, over which spread a cloth. By a sudden and smart stroke the bees may be displaced from the second hive, and will fall on the table in a lump. Take the first-hived colony and place it over them, raising it a little at the bottom, when the bees below will ascend and join it, forming one family. In moving this hive, let it be done with caution, for the combs, being at present new and brittle, are otherwise apt to fall down. It is seldom that any quarrel takes place if the business be done properly; but some persons think that a little smoke previously blown into both the hives, has a tendency to prevent fighting. Early the next morning move the hive back to its former position, when one of the Queens will have been deposed. In thus uniting swarms, the doubled colony should always occupy the first hive. As a general rule, it may be remarked, that the mode the most likely to succeed is that in which the bees are suddenly blended together, without space or opportunity for individual recognition or fighting, bee against bee; but it must be done when the first hive contains but a few combs.

In this place it may be noticed, that in an apiary where a weak and sluggish old stock is now observed, opportunity can be taken to add to its numbers, by uniting to it an after-swarm, in the mode just pointed out; though some persons would prefer puffing a little smoke to both parties. If either Queen be removed, the strangers will usually be well received, and this accession of numbers is almost certain to lead to a vastly increased action and industry.

Like most other operations on bees, the mode of uniting swarms admits of variety, according to choice and circumstance; and some apiarians prefer to drive them, in the way for which general directions have been given at page 152; a plan that may be resorted to almost at any time. Another mode of junction can be effected by the aid of a sheet of perforated zinc, inserted between the two hives about to be united. There is little reason to doubt that the members of each colony of bees are distinguishable amongst themselves by a certain peculiarity of odour, which, if assimilated, appears to have the effect of preventing mutual dissension. When the construction, therefore, of the hives admits of their being brought into juxtaposition, the perforated zinc allows a free circulation of scent between them, without permitting actual contact of the bees. After leaving matters in this position for two or three days, I have usually found, on withdrawing the zinc divider, that no disturbance has ensued.

Prevention of After-swarms.—Where the construction of the hive admits of it, no doubt the repetition of swarming may be prevented by depriving it of the royal cells. Under the head *Bar-Hives*, we have alluded to the facilities given for this object; and it may be done immediately on the issuing of a swarm, when but a small portion of the bees will remain in it. Let the cover be unscrewed, and moved sideways as required, puffing in some smoke on each side the combs, which must be lifted separately, beginning first at one end of the hive, and then the other, so as to work to the centre. Cut out the Queen cells as you proceed, replacing the bar. A quarter of an hour will suffice for the operation. In the meanwhile, the swarm may be hived in the usual way, and afterwards permanently returned; for her majesty has now no alternative; "stay at home," as Mr. Golding says, "she *must*. Or," he continues, "after the first swarm is gone off, subsequent ones may be prevented in this way: so soon as the *long* note of piping has been heard, cut away at the royal cells. The young princess, *already at liberty*, will then remain Queen of the stock."

Maiden Swarms.—Under peculiar circumstances of early season and situation, a prime swarm will occasionally send forth another, the original Queen again going with it; in such instances, termed a maiden swarm; rarely, however, of much value. "In this case," says Dr. Bevan, "it usually occurs between the twenty-eighth and thirtieth day of its establishment. The only indication of the approach of such an issue, besides those already enumerated, is the worker-combs, with which first swarms generally store their hives, becoming edged with drone-cells." Indeed, an indispensable condition necessary to a maiden swarm is a Queen, capable of producing drones; and this rarely happens in the case of a young one.

General Directions on Swarming.—An absurd custom is very general of beating a metal pan, or some such sonorous thing, usually called *tanging*, on the occasion of bee-swarming. The practice, doubtless, originated in the precaution formerly observed of ringing a bell, or giving some signal of the flight of bees, with a view to an identification of the property in case of its straying to a distance. By degrees the idea became prevalent that the bees themselves were the parties interested in the hubbub; but as regards them it is worse than useless, and frequently prevents their settling so soon as they would do if left quietly to themselves. The drenching or anointing of a hive, intended for a swarm, with any kind of material, is another common practice much better avoided. A dry clean hive is preferable; only, if of straw, cutting off the loose ends. As respects the precise mode of housing a swarm, no directions will meet all cases. After rushing in great apparent excitement from the family domicile, the bees form a cloud in the air, wheeling about in a thousand directions, and exhibiting a scene of the greatest animation; then, for the purpose of assembling together, they alight and cluster round the Queen that has accompanied them, usually on a bush or branch of a low tree. The hive must now be put close under the swarm, into which it is easily shaken; or, according to circumstances, swept with a light brush, which is all the better if made of very fine shavings; but care should be taken not to crush any bees. The success of the operation depends upon the inclusion of the Queen, when the new family will soon collect with her, within the hive, on placing this in its proper position, a little raised on one side, and shaded in some way from the sun. On the occasion of swarming, bees are seldom much inclined to use their stings, unless irritated by wind. The hiving ought not to be delayed, especially with a hot sun, or the bees would soon again take wing, perhaps for a long flight, and be hopelessly lost. A somewhat larger hive may be selected for a full-sized early swarm than for a later one. In case a swarm returns to the parent hive, which sometimes happens, let the latter be watched, for it will soon re-issue, and perhaps on the same day. Occasionally a swarm will divide and settle in two parts, which, if near together, can be shaken into one hive. Otherwise a junction may be made at night, in the way pointed out at page 193. An observance of the advice of Gelieu, and others, is to be recommended, not to allow the swarm to remain where it had been hived till the evening, as is customary, but to place it at once, as soon as settled, or within a quarter of an hour, on the spot (if at hand) it is destined to occupy. In sultry weather raise the hive a little to admit air, especially if a large swarm. When first hived, it is curious to observe the caution with which bees mark the site of their new position, making circuits in the air, wider and wider, till they clearly understand the locality. Having done this, they are much perplexed at any subsequent removal of their dwelling; nor do they ever, under ordinary circumstances, re-enter the original parent-hive.

We may say a word as to the practice of some proprietors, with a view of giving additional strength to a recent swarm: the stock-hive from whence the issue took place is moved to a little distance, and immediately that the swarm is settled in its new hive, the latter is placed on the site which the other had just left. The outlying bees, on returning home, will of course fly to the original spot, joining and strengthening the new family. The old one must necessarily be weakened in the same proportion, but it will soon be recruited by the maturation of the brood which it is sure to contain. Sometimes this shifting of the stock-hive has been allowed to be permanent; whilst, in other instances, it has been found more expedient only to do it for two or three hours immediately following the swarming. The hives should, under the latter supposition, then be made to change places, and no bees would be lost, as one or the other of the two positions would be sought by them.

It may be well to refer the reader to what has been said at page 108, relative to the occasional necessity that might exist for feeding a newly-hived family of bees.

Artificial Swarming.—Many apiculturists have practised the making of what have been termed artificial swarms of bees;—in other words, have compelled them to leave the parent hive sooner than they would have done in their own natural way. What is more common than to see a large bunch of bees hanging in idleness, often for weeks, on the outside of a stock-hive, at the best part of the season. Is it not a great gain if we can contrive in some way to set this unprofitable community to work, in a new home? The advantages of early swarms have been already pointed out, and in our uncertain climate the risk is often great, either of losing them altogether, or of their coming too late for the principal season of blossoming. Such considerations have led to the compulsory system, which may, in one form or another, often be successfully resorted to by the practised hand, but otherwise, it is scarcely to be wondered at that failure sometimes ensues. Different operators have succeeded in different ways of proceeding; and we will briefly point out some of them. The raising of a young Queen from worker larvæ has been already described under the head *Queen Bee*; and for the purpose we have now immediately in view, we will suppose the use of a bar-hive, as the one best adapted; the time of year being that when it is ascertained to contain eggs and young larvæ, both of workers and drones. A comb must be abstracted from a full box, and put into an empty one, care being taken that it is not allowed to chill during removal. In describing the subsequent process, we may adopt the words of Dr. Bevan. "Towards noon of a fine day, or almost at any time, if the bees cluster out much (for there ought to be plenty of them), let a stock-hive be removed to a distance, and a spare hive or box be put in its place, to one bar of which is attached a comb containing worker-eggs, or very young larvæ of the same sex (better still if the hive contain also one or two other worker combs); the outliers, or the bees that are abroad, or both, will then enter the new habitation, cluster round the brood, construct one or more royal cells, and raise a young sovereign: and thus, if the season be favorable, form a flourishing stock; whilst the old removed family, with beneficially reduced numbers, will soon be reconciled to their new situation." But we may often proceed a step further, and at once ensure the presence in the new hive of an embryo sovereign, by inspecting a stock about the time of closing up the royal cells, and deprive it of a comb, containing one or more of these, as alluded to under the section *Prevention of After-swarms*. In this way the double advantage will be gained of ensuring greater certainty, and saving valuable time; for, from the commencement of the process of raising a Queen from the worm, to the period at which young bees may be looked for—her progeny—can scarcely be less than seven weeks.

Artificial swarm-making is sometimes successfully accomplished by means of driving the bees; to the general principles of which process we have directed attention at page 80. A diversity in the objects to be obtained, of course, leads to a little alteration in the details of the proceedings; and we have now in view, not, as before, the creation of a young Queen in the new hive, but forcing the old one into the latter. Dr. Dunbar thus narrates his own method of procedure, and which will usually be found to answer. "We carried," says he, "the full hive into a dark place, turned it up, fixed it in the frame of a chair from which the bottom had been removed, placed an empty hive over it, mouth to mouth, and partially drove it. As soon as we perceived that about half of the bees had ascended into the empty hive (knowing that in these cases the Queen is generally amongst the foremost), we immediately replaced the old hive on its former station, and removed the new one, now containing the Queen, to a little distance. As the former had plenty of eggs and brood, they were at no loss to procure another Queen; whilst the other, having a Queen, proceeded to work in all respects as a natural swarm." To avoid annoyance, and loss of the foraging bees, as they continue to return homewards, during the process of the preceding operation, it is well to set an empty hive (or it may have a few combs) on the site just before occupied by the parent stock. The bees will be in no very placid mood, and this piece of deception has a tendency to divert their attention temporarily, till the re-establishment of their old house restores them to their proper home.

Some operators so far depart from the mode of proceeding we have described as to prefer placing the newly driven swarm, possessing the Queen, on the old site. In such case the original stock-hive is removed to a little distance, and the entrance door stopped up, but raising the bottom edge sufficiently to admit a sufficiency of air only, with but little of light or sun. The bees thus confined are left undisturbed during two days, and will probably have spent their time in founding a prospective new monarchy. They may then be safely again trusted abroad, for in their anxiety about the requirements of the provisional government, they will no more trouble their old companions. Another variation of plan, recommended by some, is, instead of shutting up either portion of the bees, immediately to convey those driven into the new hive, to a distance of not less than a mile, leaving the original position for the old one.[AC]

[AC] I may here not inappropriately call attention to a subject touched upon by Mr. Golding. His remarks are borne out by my own observation; and I believe it would be for mutual benefit were bee-keepers, resident a few miles apart, occasionally to exchange swarms in the season. I make no apology for introducing a passage from the 'Shilling Bee-Book.' "Though I can give no satisfactory reasons for the fact, yet it certainly is one, that bees brought from a distance very generally thrive better than families long domiciled on the spot. I am borne out in this opinion by the concurrent testimony of my apiarian friends. Whether they ply more vigorously on finding themselves in a strange situation, or what can be the reason, I leave others to guess at." An American author observes on this subject, "I am strongly persuaded that the decay of many stocks may be attributed to the fact that the bees have become enfeebled by *close breeding*. The cultivator should guard against this evil by occasionally changing his stocks."

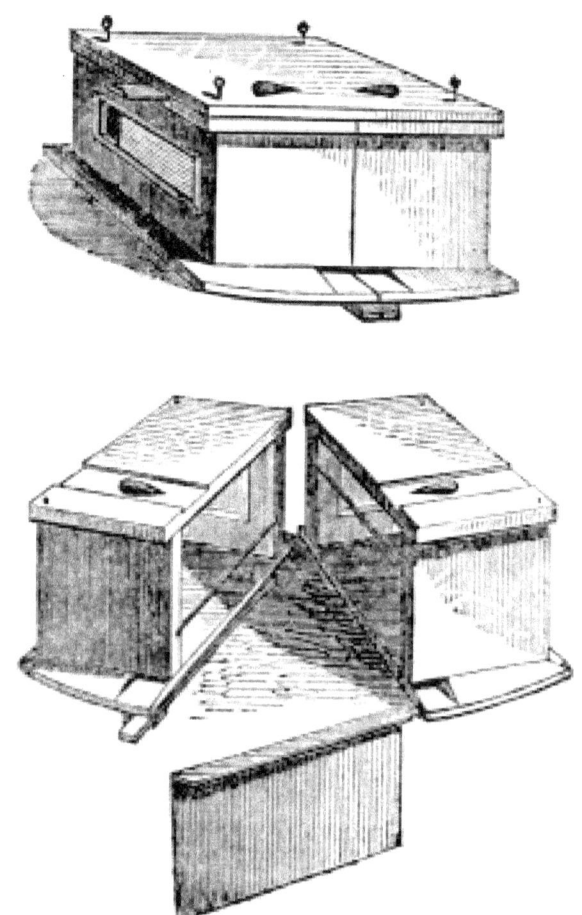

Dividing Bar-Hive.—So far we are supposed to have proceeded in forcing artificial swarms with hives of the usual kind. But an idea has often been suggested of having boxes so made as to be divisible vertically into equal halves; and, in this way, to create the basis of two distinct families without swarming. Such hives are alluded to by various authors, and, amongst them, by Dr. Dunbar and Dr. Bevan; but we have hitherto had no guide as to any intelligible details of construction; and on these depends the possibility of proceeding with advantage. My own views on the subject induced me to think that my eight-bar hive, already described, possessed, with a little modification, the required facilities; and, indeed, I know of no other that could be so adapted. Moreover, as the original dimensions are preserved, the other boxes and all adjuncts remain as detailed at p. 54, so that the hive can be used without reference to the provision made for subdividing it; this being altogether a super-added advantage. The chief novelty is in the stock-box, which, with its cover, is cut from front to back into two equal parts, but so as not to alter the regular interspacing of the bars, four of which will of course appertain to each compartment. In addition to the usual side-windows, there should be a small one at the back of both the half-boxes. The hive-board must also be divided, so as to be lifted up each half independently of the other. Cross bars are appended on the underneath side of the boards, the ends meeting in the centre. A groove is here notched out from the upper side of the extremities of the cross bars, to receive a moveable tongue, as it may be called, of half-inch wood and an inch wide, inserted from behind, and passing through to the front. The tongue connects the half-boards together on one level, and forms a joint below. The entrance for the bees is in the centre,

—half being cut out of each board; though, probably, some persons might prefer to have, instead, a smaller one at the two outer extremities. In order to stiffen and serve as a stay or tie at the divided ends, I have found the utility of a piece of very strong tinned wire, crossing each half-box, horizontally. All that is needed is to cut the wire into the requisite lengths, turn the ends at a right angle, and drive them flush into the wood; where, as they fall within the space between the two central bars, they are not at all in the way. A reference to the illustration will be found sufficiently explanatory, the two half-boxes being shown a little separated. When placed together, to form one hive, they are held in position by means of the centre-board, covering the whole top, and secured at the four corners by means of iron pins going down through the centre-board and the projecting edge of the crown-board of the boxes. On the occasion of hiving a swarm, for the purpose of stocking the dividing-hive, a cord or strap must be passed round the whole, and guide-combs should be used; for successful subsequent separation of the two halves depends altogether upon the regular working of the combs in straight lines upon the bars.

It will naturally occur, that to carry out the design of a *Dividing Hive* every part must have its duplicate, so that four halves, boards, &c., are necessary; each made so precisely alike as to fit and be attached to any other half-box. We must suppose the time of year to be arrived (usually in May) when the combs are well filled with brood, both of worker and drone bees. In the middle, or, as some would prefer, the evening, of a fine day, the two halves of the hive can be separated. To effect this with as little disturbance as possible, two *dividers* may be used. These are made of strong, well-flattened sheet zinc or tin, the full size of the box, in length; and deep enough to include the hive-board, besides an inch at the top edge to spare. This latter part should be turned back, as a rim or flanch, at a right angle, as seen in the illustration. Commence by withdrawing the wooden tongue underneath the hive-board, and removing the centre-board; then, with a thin knife-blade, the half-boxes can be loosened at their point of junction; not allowing the knife to enter beyond the thickness of the wood. This done, gently insert one of the dividing plates horizontally from behind, its whole length; there being no obstruction, unless the combs are worked across the bars. The other divider is to be pushed in in a similar way, the flanches resting respectively right and left on the upper edge of each half-box. The latter may then be moved apart on their boards in safety. An empty half-box is to be adjusted to each of the full halves, when the dividers may be withdrawn. We have thus two families, which must be moved some distance apart. The Queen will, of course, be in one of them; and, probably, Queen larvæ in the other, or in both halves. A little tapping will serve to show the position of the Queen, as the bees will soon become quiet where she is, whilst in the queenless box confusion will continue to prevail. The latter should then be put on the original stand, to receive the foraging bees as they return home; whilst the presence of the old Queen will secure a sufficiency in the other hive, which may be placed at a little distance. In about twenty-four hours, preparation will have commenced for founding one or more royal cells, if required, in the queenless half-hive; and thus a new colony will arise, without swarming.[AD]

[AD] The dividing hive, and some other inventions described in the 'Bee-keeper's Manual,' may be seen at Messrs. Neighbour and Sons, 127, High Holborn, and 149, Regent Street, London.

BEE-PROTECTOR.

It ought to be remarked that, in general, all important operations on bees should be conducted in the middle of the day, that being the time when it is least annoying to them, and the safest to the operator, as a large portion are then engaged abroad. Indeed, the bees are always more suspicious and irascible by night. On their homeward way they are not disposed to attack, any more than they are when at work in the fields. The defence of *home* is their actuating principle; and the danger arises from the bees furiously darting out on any supposed enemy, from within the hive. Make as little bustle and disturbance as possible, and have at hand an assistant and whatever is likely to be wanted, for a very trifling matter will often mar an operation irretrievably. Let all things be done coolly and quietly, and without hurried motions of any kind, which cause suspicion and irritation. Avoid breathing on the bees; and, above all, be careful to kill none, for the smell of the wounded body exasperates them exceedingly: in short, the aim should be to do what is needed without the bees being conscious of it. Another precaution may be mentioned, which is, in operating, not to employ any one known to be obnoxious to bees; for without going the length of saying with some that certain individuals are recognised by them, it is well known that, from their nice discrimination of scent, the persons of others are objects of constant and very marked dislike.

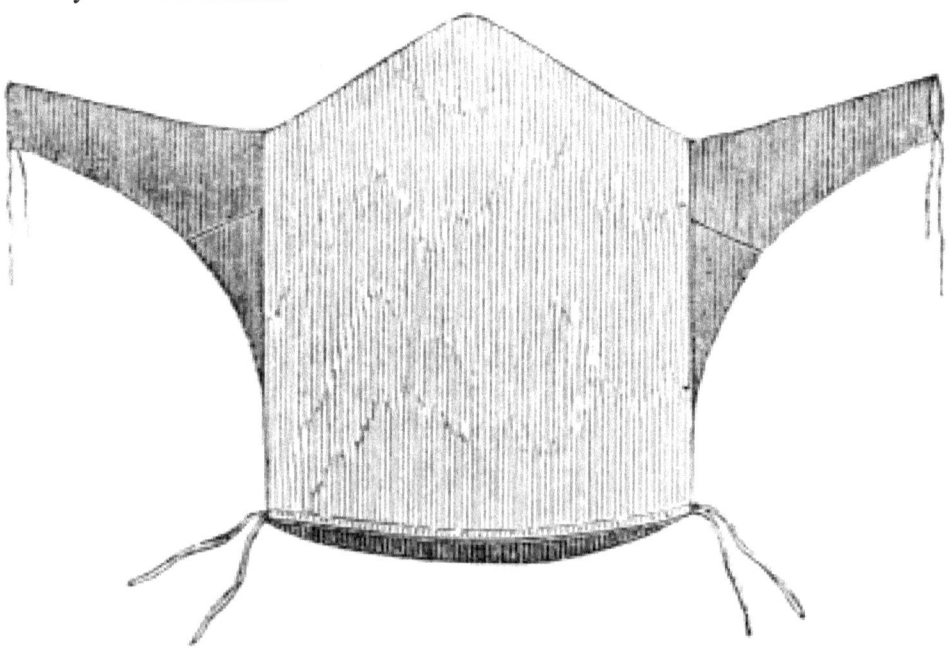

Security from attack, however, is essential to self-possession, and I know of no covering so effectual as an envelope I devised of a kind of light net, or gauze, sometimes called *leno*. It should be so made at the top as to go over a hat or cap; with sleeves, tied at the wrists, and strings at the bottom to draw and fasten round the waist. The sleeves may be made of some stronger material. (See preceding page.) The entire upper part of the person is in this way enveloped, as seen in our engraving annexed. The projection of the hat keeps the dress clear of the face, and it is sufficiently transparent. A thick pair of gloves, which some think are best made of buck-skin, is all that is further necessary to complete protection.

REMEDY FOR THE STING OF A BEE.

If attacked by a bee, the best plan is not to offer resistance, but to walk away and thrust your head into a neighbouring shrub or bush, when the enemy will in all probability retire. However, an accidental sting may now and then be received, for which various remedies have been prescribed. In the first place, the sting should at once be removed, but without rubbing the part. My own experience leads me to recommend, in preference to anything else, the immediate application of *liquor potassæ* to the spot, as a powerful alkali, to neutralize the poison of the sting, which is an acid. It should be used in small quantity, on a point of some kind, as a needle, introduced into the wound. In the absence of this, *pure liquid ammonia* is said on good authority to succeed, if properly applied. Keep it in a close-stopped, small-necked bottle, which should be turned bottom upwards, and held very tight over the part. Some persons have found relief from an immediate application of cold water. Indeed, any remedy to be efficacious must be speedily resorted to; and particularly in the warm months, for then the poison is much more active than in winter.

CONCLUSION.

In the foregoing pages I have given an outline of my own experience in the general management of bees, freely availing myself of such further information, derived from the most trustworthy sources, as seemed most likely to interest and instruct the reader. My aim, however, has been restricted primarily to matters of a *practical* bearing, passing over the obsolete speculations of by-gone periods, and relying on the superior intelligence of a later day. Those who wish to enter more fully into the natural history and physiology of the bee may consult a variety of works, at the head of which it is usual to place that of Huber; followed by the later comprehensive and highly satisfactory one, 'The Honey Bee,' of the late Dr. Bevan; both publications to which we have often had occasion to refer. That portion of the subject relating to the structure and arrangement of their combs and cells is treated of at considerable length by Lord Brougham, in his 'Dissertations on Subjects of Science connected with Natural Theology.' Perhaps the accurate observations and elaborate mathematical demonstrations of the noble author have left little more to be desired in the particular department to which he has devoted the energies of his powerful mind. With his summary of the progress of apiarian knowledge, we may not inappropriately close the 'Bee-keeper's Manual.'

"The attention," says Lord Brougham,[AE] "which has been paid at various times to the structure and habits of the bee is one of the most remarkable circumstances in the history of science. The ancients studied it with unusual minuteness, although being, generally speaking, indifferent observers of fact, they made but little progress in discovering the singular economy of this insect. Of the observations of Aristomachus, who spent sixty years, it is said, in studying the subject, we know nothing; nor of those which were made by Philissus, who passed his life in the woods, for the purpose of examining this insect's habits; but Pliny informs us that both of them wrote works upon it. Aristotle's three chapters on bees and wasps[AF] contain little more than the ordinary observations, mixed up with an unusual portion of vulgar and even gross errors. How much he attended to the subject is, however, manifest from the extent of the first of these chapters, which is of great length. Some mathematical writers, particularly Pappus, studied the form of the cells, and established one or two of the fundamental propositions respecting the economy of labour and wax resulting from the plan of the structure. The application of modern naturalists to the inquiry is to be dated from the beginning of the eighteenth century, when Maraldi examined it with his accustomed care; and Reaumur afterwards, as we have seen, carried his investigations much farther. The interest of the subject seemed to increase with the progress made in their inquiries; and about the year 1765 a society was formed at Little Bautzen in Upper Lusatia, whose sole object was the study of bees. It was formed under the patronage of the Elector of Saxony. The celebrated Schirach was one of its original members; and soon after its establishment he made his famous discovery of the power which the bees have to supply the loss of their Queen, by forming a large cell out of three common ones, and feeding the grub of a worker upon royal jelly; a discovery so startling to naturalists, that Bonnet, in 1769, earnestly urged the society not to lower its credit by countenancing such a wild error, which he regarded as repugnant to all we know of the habits of insects; admitting, however, that he should not be so incredulous of any observations tending to prove the propagation of the race of the Queen-bee, without any co-operation of a male,[AG] a notion since shown by Huber to be wholly chimerical. In 1771 a second institution, with the same limited object, was founded at Lauter, under the Elector Palantine's patronage, and of this Riem, scarcely less known in this branch of science than Schirach, was a member.

[AE] Vol. i, pp. 333-36.

[AF] Hist. An., lib. ix, cap. 40, 41, 42.

[AG] Œuvres, x, 100, 104.

"The greatest progress, however, was afterwards made by Huber, whose discoveries, especially of the Queen-bee's mode of impregnation, the slaughter of the drones or males, and the mode of working, have justly gained him a very high place among naturalists. Nor are his discoveries of the secretion of wax from saccharine matter, the nature of propolis, and the preparation of wax, for building, to be reckoned less important. To these truths the way had been led by John Hunter, whose vigorous and original genius never was directed to the cultivation of any subject without reaping a harvest of discovery."

In conclusion, whatever may be the degree of ignorance or doubt in which on certain points respecting the Honey-bee we are still involved (and these are probably not often practically important), there are few but may receive instruction and example from these wonderful little creatures, in the duties of persevering industry, prudence, economy, and peaceful subordination; whilst all may be taught, by their perfect organization and faultless adaptation of means to an end, a lesson of humility; and, finally, by the contemplation of their beautiful works, "to look from Nature up to Nature's God."